THE
GIRLS

THE GIRLS

An All-American Town, a Predatory Doctor,
and the Untold Story of the Gymnasts
Who Brought Him Down

ABIGAIL PESTA

SEAL PRESS

NEW YORK

Seal Press

Hachette Book Group

1290 Avenue of the Americas, New York, NY 10104

www.sealpress.com

@sealpress

Printed in the United States of America

First Edition: August 2019

Published by Seal Press, an imprint of Perseus Books, LLC, a subsidiary of Hachette Book Group, Inc. The Seal Press name and logo is a trademark of the Hachette Book Group.

The Hachette Speakers Bureau provides a wide range of authors for speaking events. To find out more, go to www.hachettespeakersbureau.com or call (866) 376-6591.

The publisher is not responsible for websites (or their content) that are not owned by the publisher.

Print book interior design by Amnet Systems.

Library of Congress Cataloging-in-Publication Data has been applied for.

ISBNs: 978-1-58005-880-3 (hardcover), 978-1-58005-881-0 (ebook)

LSC-C

Printing 3, 2022

Author's Note

This project is a work of original reporting based on interviews that I conducted with twenty-five survivors of more than a quarter century of abuse and manipulation at the hands of Larry Nassar. Many of the women I interviewed—including the woman who may have been his very first target—are publicly sharing an extended, personal account of their childhood abuse and the aftermath for the first time in the pages of this book. To reveal Nassar's evolution from doctor to predator, I also interviewed family members, coaches, legal experts, and many others, and collected and reviewed hundreds of pages of court documents and police records spanning the decades.

To the army of survivors.
To my team: Joel, Mom, Dad, and Jesse.

Contents

Forward, Together

*By Tasha Schwikert, US Olympic Team medalist, and
Jordan Schwikert, US National Team member*

At first we found it hard to believe. Larry Nassar, the famous Olympic Team doctor, had been accused of sexually abusing young girls. We thought, What? Larry? No way. He was the good guy. The one who listened. The one who cared. The one who slipped us secret treats, like granola bars. Amid all the brutal coaching and training in gymnastics, he was our trusted friend.

It didn't immediately register that he had abused us too. It took some time. It's a strange feeling when you come to realize, as an adult, that you were abused as a child. Especially when the abuser is your doctor, the person who is supposed to have your best interests at heart. It was difficult to grasp that this had happened to us. As gymnasts, we had been taught to be tough. We were so mentally and physically strong, we thought that no one could take advantage of us. We were the most resilient athletes around.

We weren't alone in our initial disbelief. Many of the women he abused as children had a hard time believing he had abused them.

This tends to surprise people; they assume we all knew we had been abused but had kept it quiet. But many of us did not know. He was the Olympic doctor. He said he was doing a medical treatment. We trusted him.

The two of us grew up putting our faith in coaches and doctors. They were our world. We started gymnastics as toddlers, going to Mommy and Me classes with our mom in our hometown of Las Vegas. She encouraged us to try different sports—soccer, T-ball, tennis. She had been a serious athlete herself, a tennis player who had made it to Wimbledon. But we loved gymnastics. When Mom took us to play tennis, we ended up doing cartwheels and backflips all over the court. We just wanted to go to the gym. We had found our passion.

We're pretty close in age, just a year and nine months apart, and we progressed in the sport together. Our parents let us pursue our dream. They were dice dealers at Caesars Palace, and Mom would drop us off at the gym and take a nap there before heading to work. Our coach, Cassie Rice, was young and just starting out, and she was great. Her goal was to make us the best athletes—and the best people—we could be. That was more important to her than any awards or accomplishments. If we had a bad day, she encouraged us and lifted us up. She was all about positive reinforcement.

When we started winning state competitions, people noticed. In the midnineties, we got invited to join the Talent Opportunity Program, known as TOPs, a training program for promising young gymnasts run by USA Gymnastics, the governing body for the sport and for the US Olympic Team. As part of the program, we qualified for the TOPs national training camp, held in Tulsa, Oklahoma. There, the days were long and tiring. The coaches at the camp also coached the US National Team, so we got a taste of what it takes to reach the elite level of the sport. We actually looked forward to the camp's nutrition class because we could escape the relentless training. Not that the nutrition class was very helpful—we were just told what not to eat. That was the first time we started thinking about food in a negative way.

By our early teens, we had climbed to the elite level. When we made the US National Team, the training got toxic. We spent a lot of time at the Karolyi Ranch, the official training center for the National Team, based in Texas. We dreaded going there. The coaching was all negative—verbally and emotionally abusive. It was a terrible, threatening environment, all about power and control. As soon as you stepped into that gym, you became a robot. You weren't allowed to be exhausted, to be human. You turned off your emotions. If you got injured, the coaches made you feel useless, so everyone hid their injuries and kept training, taking medications to mask the pain. We saw girls get so tired, they nearly landed on their heads while doing skills, yet they were ordered to repeat those skills again and again. It was dangerous, with coaches pushing us way past the point of fatigue. None of us had a voice. To speak out meant angering the coaches and losing your standing. It was such an extreme environment, Aly Raisman once said she was scared to ask for a bar of soap.

Our parents weren't allowed at the Karolyi Ranch. But Larry Nassar was there. He was always on hand for the training camps at the ranch, and he became a best friend. We could go to him and be human. His training room was our safe place; the door would shut, and we would confide our problems without worrying that we would get in trouble. That's how he drew us in.

For me, Tasha speaking here, the abuse started when I was fifteen, after an incident at the ranch. We were all doing the "oversplits," splits in which you elevate one or both of your feet, forcing your body to go down deeper than the regular splits. Coach Bela Karolyi pushed me down too hard, but I held back my tears. I had just watched Bela shouting at Jamie Dantzscher, calling her a "baby," and I didn't want to get yelled at myself. The next day, limping from pain in my groin area, I got sent to Larry. He massaged and penetrated me vaginally with his bare hands, claiming it was a medical treatment that would loosen my muscles. I trusted him because he was a respected doctor, and I had known him for years. Also, it's important to note that in gymnastics, you're extremely isolated. I didn't know about sexual abuse. And you spend so many hours of your life in training at the gym, there's no time for dating or socializing. I had no experience with boys or sex. None of us did.

When I was seventeen, I had an Achilles injury that became so bad I could barely walk. Larry told my mom that he had a week when his schedule wasn't crazy. Then he made a phenomenal offer: he said he could treat me at his home in Lansing, Michigan, for the week. He told me to ask my mother if she would buy me a plane ticket to Lansing and said I could stay with him and his family. I desperately needed to get back on my feet, and I appreciated his thoughtful gesture. This important doctor was making all this time for me. I thought, Wow, as a top athlete, I'm getting the LeBron James treatment. And so I went and stayed with Larry, his wife, and his children for five days. They made me feel right at home. It was like staying with family, like visiting a trusted uncle. He worked on me every day, either in his basement, where he kept a massage table and medical supplies, or at an athletic training room at Michigan State University, where he also worked. He did an MRI, acupuncture, electrical nerve stimulation, and ultrasound. Every session was accompanied by a massage. He would start by massaging my Achilles tendon and would work his way up my leg, eventually penetrating me. He said, "Everything is connected," claiming that applying pressure to one part of my body would help another. He performed this abusive "treatment" on me three times a day—morning, noon, and night.

Looking back, I remember hearing girls sometimes say, "Does Larry creep you out?" But we would all brush it off, saying, "Nah, he's just nerdy Larry." We had been taught not to question, not to make any noise. The officials at USA Gymnastics told us to smile, to make everything look effortless, glamorous. When we got trained on how to talk to the media, we were told, "Talk about how great it is to be an elite gymnast." We were supposed to make it all seem like rainbows and butterflies. We were expected to be the perfect, obedient athletes. It's like a job, and if you make a misstep, you are highly aware that you're replaceable—you are often reminded of that. When the officials at USA Gymnastics picked me for the Olympic Team in 2000, I felt grateful. I was one of just six girls on the team that year. Yes, I had worked hard, but I felt deeply indebted too. I won an Olympic medal and owed my success to USA Gymnastics.

More than a decade later, after the allegations of abuse made the news, I got a call from Steve Penny, then the president of USA Gymnastics. At the time, I had just finished law school and was busy studying for the bar exam, which was days away and all-consuming. I was also raising my first child and soon to be pregnant with my second. My husband, a pro basketball player, played overseas with his team, so I was on my own. I hadn't had a single second to process the allegations of abuse or think about whether it had happened to me. I had to stay focused and not get derailed. Steve Penny blindsided me by asking whether I had been abused. With no time to think about how to answer, I heard myself saying no. Then he asked me to sign a statement in support of both Larry and USA Gymnastics. He knew I still felt grateful, which is why he targeted me. Under pressure, I agreed to sign a statement supporting USA Gymnastics, but not Larry. USA Gymnastics blasted the statement out on Twitter, with a picture of me at the world championships.

Finally, after I passed the bar exam, started a job at a law firm, and had my second child, I had time to face the skeletons in my closet. I looked back through my memories and started putting the puzzle pieces together. Larry's manipulative tactics came into focus. It was mortifying to realize that this had really happened to

me. I wrestled emotionally with the fact that I had been so manipulated. Me, the strong, impermeable African American athlete. I
beat myself up about it. I kept thinking, I should have known; I
should have known. I spent a lot of time with my therapist on that.
I couldn't see at first that the blame was on him, not me, for using
his position as the Olympic doctor to take advantage of children.
The adults I trusted as a kid to keep me safe—not just Larry, but
also the officials at USA Gymnastics—had profoundly let me down.
They had failed to protect me.

I thought about the many ways Larry had built up our friendship and trust when we were young girls. He would often ask
about our personal lives, about our boy crushes. We all had little
crushes on guys on the men's team, or on boy-band pop singers.
We thought Larry was in our inner circle. I didn't realize as a child
how inappropriate it was that a grown man was so interested and
involved in these conversations. Other moments of manipulation
came back to me too. I remembered how at one of the national
championship qualifying meets, I was leaving the training room
after a "treatment" from Larry and another gymnast was coming
in. Larry told the other gymnast he had just done this "treatment"
on me that had worked. At the time, I was one of the top-ranked
gymnasts in the United States, and this girl looked up to me. I
can see now that he used me to establish her trust. A sickening
realization.

For me, Jordan speaking here, the abuse began when I was in
my early teens and started training at the Karolyi Ranch, where
I suffered injuries from the relentless pounding and repetitive
stress, eventually leading to a major back injury. Because Larry
was a world-renowned doctor, I thought he must know the best
medical techniques. I assumed his invasive procedure was something he did to treat my specific injuries—I never imagined that
he did it to everyone. I had no clue that he gave Tasha the same
"treatment." We never talked about it. I knew nothing about sexual

abuse. I had always thought of it as something more violent, like a rapist holding you down, not something your doctor would do while pretending to help you. Now I know that abusers are often very close personally to the people they target. But back then, I was a kid in an insane universe where you couldn't say if you were injured or hungry. I had learned early on not to make the mistake of saying I was hurt; once, when I did, I got banished to a back gym at the ranch for the day. That was the worst. You never wanted to fall off "the good list."

Years later, when I first heard the allegations of abuse, I felt confused; I couldn't imagine that Larry would hurt anyone. I was engaged to be married at the time, busy planning my wedding. It wasn't until I started reading more details in the news and connecting personally with other gymnasts that I began to realize, Wow, their stories sound very similar to mine. That's when it all came to light. His hand had been in my vagina, and not for medical reasons. I felt disgusted. At first, honestly, I wanted to block it out. As the scandal kept growing, I went to Tasha and said, "You know, he touched me in a weird way too." We were both surprised to hear that it had happened to the other. It was a hard conversation to have.

Now I'm a gymnastics coach, and I have an opportunity to help change the culture of the sport that allowed this abuse to go on for decades. Recently I sat down with the girls I coach, telling them, "If you ever feel weird or uncertain about anything, speak up." I want them to know that they can come to me and talk about whatever they want, that they have a voice. I know that kids often have a hard time communicating with adults or don't have the confidence to do so. I want to create a safe, encouraging, positive environment for them, and I keep a watchful eye.

There are many things that people have yet to understand about the Nassar nightmare. This book answers the questions people so often ask. How did this doctor get away with decades of sexual abuse? How did he become such a master predator? Why didn't parents know? Why didn't many kids tell? And when kids *did* know and *did* tell—which a number of kids did—why didn't officials listen? There were plenty of times when this man could have been stopped. Why weren't these young athletes and their families protected? Who are the people and institutions who failed these girls and enabled this monster?

The deeply personal stories and astounding insights from the people in these pages, many of whom grew up with Larry Nassar in their close-knit community in Michigan, shed crucial light on all of this—and will help prevent this kind of travesty from happening again.

We share our own story with that same goal.

—As told to Abigail Pesta

Tasha Schwikert is a 2000 Olympic bronze medalist, a two-time national champion, and a graduate of UCLA, where she won many titles on the gymnastics team. Jordan Schwikert competed on the US National Team from 2001 to 2002 and later on the UCLA team, where she was named Gymnast of the Year in 2008, the year she graduated.

Chapter One

The Dream

Sara Teristi saw the making of a monster. She watched a man transform from doctor to predator, starting decades ago when he gained access to a gym full of little girls. She was one of those girls. She may have been his very first target.

Her fateful march toward Larry Nassar—the most prolific sex criminal in American sports history—began when she was in kindergarten, a typical kid growing up in a tiny town along the banks of the Grand River in Michigan. As an only child, she liked to entertain herself by looking for turtles, cattails, and puffball mushrooms in a creek near her home. These were the days before cell phones and i-things, and she and her friends often played outside until dusk, when their parents would ring a cowbell to call them home for dinner. The kids played tag in the yard or ghost in the graveyard in an actual graveyard, jumping out to scare each other from behind the tombstones. If the streetlights came on and Sara hadn't heard the clank of the cowbell, she knew it was time to head home. At night, she slept beneath a poster of rock star Pat Benatar.

Her town, Dimondale, was so small, it didn't need any stoplights. Just a few miles from the city of Lansing, the town made a name for itself back in the sixties for its horseshoe-pitching prowess, producing champion pitchers. Some people called it "the horseshoe capital of the world." Today, people paddle down the river in kayaks and canoes, shop at the farmers' market.

As a child, Sara lived just outside town, in a neighborhood known as Copville because of its proximity to the police post. Several cops lived in the area, her father among them. When her dad would come home from work, looking for a little peace and quiet, Sara would be bouncing around the house, bursting with energy. An exuberant kid, she had a hard time sitting still, especially when Dad came home in his state trooper uniform. And so, in September 1980, when she was five years old, her mother enrolled her in a gymnastics class, hoping she could burn off some energy there.

The class was part of a youth gymnastics program at Michigan State University, in nearby East Lansing. Sara's mom would drive her there on Saturdays in her powder-blue Datsun 210, and Sara, wearing her auburn hair in braids like Laura Ingalls from *Little House on the Prairie*, would bound into the gym in her leotard. She embraced the sport. If anything, it made her more energetic, not less. She cartwheeled up and down the halls of her family's ranch house, rattling vases and photo frames. She did handstands against the door of the coat closet, causing the dog to bark like crazy in confusion. She used her bed as a trampoline, bouncing so high, she scraped her nose on the ceiling. In class at the gym, she learned how to master the balance beam and uneven bars, how to spin and flip and fly.

Over the next few years, she moved up to an advanced group and began practicing alongside girls more than twice her age. Her coach was hard-driving, serious. If Sara was afraid to learn a new skill, he would order her to go stand in a corner. She understood. There was no room for fear if you wanted to be a good gymnast. Plus, standing in the corner was embarrassing, so she would try again until she got it right. In 1984, when she was ten years old, her coach recommended that she try out for a spot at a gymnastics club in Lansing called Great Lakes Gymnastics. "They can take you to the next level," he said. At private clubs such as this one, scattered across the country, girls can train to compete in state, national, and sometimes international meets. They can get on track for a college scholarship. Or maybe, for a lucky few, the Olympics. Jordyn Wieber, who won Olympic gold with her team in 2012, grew up in a town just down the road from Dimondale. There is always the dream.

Sara wanted to go for it. Still, she was nervous about the prospect of joining the new club. For a couple of nights before the tryouts, she lay awake in bed, trying to will herself to sleep. When she arrived for the big day, she was surprised at the scene: the gym was tucked away in a musty old warehouse, with plastic buckets strewn about the floor, catching drips from the leaky ceiling. The grim place was a far cry from the gleaming gym at Michigan State, stocked with shiny new equipment. But there was an ambitious coach at this new gym, John Geddert, who had competed as a gymnast at Central Michigan University and then coached at a top gymnastics club, Marvateens Gymnastics, in Maryland, before returning to Michigan, where he grew up. Sara wanted to learn from him. He was gaining a reputation for training stellar athletes. Indeed, he would one day become a head coach for the 2012 US Olympic Team. Over the years, he would coach more than twenty US National Team members and help gymnasts secure more than $7 million worth of college scholarships, according to his LinkedIn page. But for many girls, it would come at a high price.

When Sara met him, John Geddert was just getting going in his career. She recalls stepping into the gym, walking past a lineup of photos on the walls—girls with scholarships. She imagined herself getting her own scholarship one day. All she had to do was survive this gym. At the tryouts, John's wife, Kathryn, one of several coaches on hand, guided her, asking her to perform a range of difficult skills. Sara knew that the coaches would want to see whether she was scared to do hard things. She showed no fear. She leaped and twirled her way through the tryouts. Afterward, she waited.

A few seemingly endless days later, she heard the news: she had been accepted. It was the happiest day of her young life.

Little did she know, she was about to go down the rabbit hole into a surreal universe in which she would lose sight of her boundaries, her body, herself.

Sara tells me this story on a misty spring day in Raleigh, North Carolina, where she lives now. We sit in a pebbled outdoor courtyard at an art museum, a quiet, serene setting she chose because she does not want to tell this story in her house. She doesn't want this tale anywhere near her home, her children. She is nervous about telling it. This is the first time she has confided in anyone, aside from her husband, about the depths of her childhood experience. She hopes that by sharing her life story for the first time in this book, she will help people understand how predators hunt their prey. Her goal is to protect children in the future. She is in her early forties now, a mother of two young boys. She wears a metal knee brace from old gymnastics injuries. Physical pain is a part of her everyday life, as it has been for decades. And then there are the psychological scars.

"People don't understand how many broken girls it takes to produce an elite athlete," she says, delivering the haunting words while sitting with the perfect posture of an athlete. "A coach can easily go through three hundred girls or more."

At Great Lakes Gymnastics, Sara entered a new world—a boot camp. The training was far more intense than at her previous gym, where she had practiced just one day a week. Here, she attended three practices a week after school, each lasting for three hours or more. Still, she welcomed the challenge. She wanted to prove she could hack it, especially since the new gym was more expensive for her parents, who both worked and were not wealthy. She wanted to help repay them with a college scholarship. They were making a lot of sacrifices so she could pursue her passion, and she knew it.

Sara begins to get emotional as she tells me this, then quickly regroups and continues. When the coaches yelled at her during practice, which they often did, she says, she would strive to do better. She especially wanted to please John Geddert. A muscular, domineering man with a strong, chiseled jaw, he exuded confidence and power. Sara knew he could carry her far in the sport if she impressed him. She became focused on making John proud. (The girls at the gym all called him by his first name, and so I am doing so here as well.)

She soon learned that he was hard to please. He intimidated the young gymnasts, ruling by fear. "He would throw clipboards at the girls if they messed up," she tells me. "He would call them worthless." Her first experience with his temper, she recalls, came when she was trying to do a roundoff / back handspring / back tuck. She took off poorly and ended up landing on her head, getting a rug burn on her face. "He was supposed to spot me," which could have prevented the fall, she says. "But he was angry that I had started off wrong. He turned his back and walked away." She got up alone, her face throbbing. Instead of being mad at her coach for failing to spot her, she was mad at herself. Lesson learned, she thought: it was her fault. The coaches often yelled at the girls for not concentrating or trying hard enough. Injuries meant you weren't focusing. If you got hurt, the blame was on you.

I sought comment from John Geddert, via his attorneys, on the experiences Sara and other gymnasts shared in this book but did not receive a response.

A light rain begins to fall as Sara speaks. We move our chairs under the branches of a leafy tree for cover, then continue our conversation as the rain drips around us. Sara recalls how the girls learned to hide injuries from their coaches. "If you said you were hurt, you would be called a liar," she recalls. She saw girls training with bloody sores on their hands, with broken fingers and toes. She got used to seeing things like that. She got used to the shouting, the insults from coaches.

"You're not trying!"

"You're useless!"

"You're lazy!"

She also learned the consequences if she didn't perform perfectly—extra laps and leg lifts repeated time and again, until she thought she would collapse. Body weight was another stress point. The coaches weighed the girls regularly, and if they didn't "make weight," they would be sentenced to running laps around the parking lot in their leotards. Sara remembers the humiliation of running around the parking lot in public, on display as a young girl in her skintight bodysuit, with cars driving by and honking, guys catcalling.

Sometimes she was ridiculed inside the gym as well. For instance, when she did handsprings, she had a hard time keeping her legs together due to a birth defect that made her legs curve slightly outward. She remembers John mocking her, making sexual jokes with another coach. "He said the boys would love me because I couldn't keep my legs together," she says. "I was just ten years old, but I knew what that meant." She felt mortified as the two men snickered, her face turning a deep red. She didn't know what to say; she was a child.

She tried to avoid John's wrath. He could be volatile and fearsome, she says, recalling a day when she didn't do well on the vault at practice. He took it out on her, getting physical. "As I was sprinting at full speed down the vault runway to try again, he shoved me midsprint," she says. "I tripped and went flying sideways, landing on the steel cables supporting the uneven bars." Bruised, she got up to try again, feeling ashamed, blaming herself.

Sara didn't tell her parents about the rough treatment at the gym because as far as she knew, this was the norm if you wanted to become a top gymnast. She had no frame of reference. She trusted the adults around her. All of it just made her more driven to impress her coach.

Looking back today, Sara describes the experience as "brain-washing." She was a young girl; John was an adult man. The power dynamic was imbalanced. If she did not please him, he could choose to ignore her instead of helping her advance. He had all the control. If she didn't perform well, he made her feel like she was nothing. She felt she could never do enough to earn his respect, so she became obsessed with trying to get it. "I was a perfection-ist," she says. "And he was a drill sergeant." As her world grew ever more focused on gymnastics, everything became about him and his opinion of her. "I would've done anything to make John happy," she says. "Eventually, I saw him more than I saw my own parents. Any child wants to make the adults in their life happy."

She began training for five hours on Saturdays in addition to the three after-school practices. The gym moved to a new space, but it wasn't much better than the old: a rented gymnasium in an empty high school that was stifling hot in the summer, with no air conditioning. To try to stay cool, Sara would take ice-cold show-ers when she got home, then stand naked in front of a fan to dry off. "One day, after five or six hours of practice, the heat really got to me," she recalls. "I felt dizzy, so I asked one of the coaches if I could go to the bathroom." She walked into the restroom and lay down on the floor, hoping she wouldn't get yelled at for taking a break. She got busted immediately. "John came in and said, 'You're faking it. Get up!'" she says. "He always walked in on the girls in the bathroom. If he noticed you weren't in the gym, he'd go searching for you in the bathroom."

She had no privacy. In retrospect, she says, this is part of how she began to lose a sense of boundaries.

To keep up with the demands of training and school, she became extremely regimented, doing homework late into the night. She sought perfection at school, just as she did in sports, and always made the honor roll. "If I got anything less than an A, I freaked out," she says. As she tells her story, I'm surprised to hear about her fierce drive at such a young age. So often you hear that parents are the ones who push their children into elite sports. Not so for Sara. She pushed herself. Her parents were proud of her, she says, but they just wanted her to be happy; they didn't force her into hours of hard-core training each week. In fact, they worried that it was getting rather overwhelming. She was sacrificing social activities and slumber parties to keep up with all the training and schoolwork. But as far as her parents knew, Sara loved the sport, and so they believed all was well. She never told them otherwise. She didn't mention how her coaches belittled her, made sexual remarks, or threw things at the girls. She thought it was just the way top coaches behaved. This isolated little universe was the only one she knew. She told herself, Suck it up. Endure. This is what it takes to be the best.

As she moved through middle school, she won state-level competitions and placed among the top three athletes in five-state regionals. John began picking her to go to all the important "away" meets. She enjoyed traveling around the country for competitions. She shares with me a funny essay she wrote as a kid about an incident at one of the meets—a glimpse of the good times amid the rigors of training:

> It was about one o'clock in the morning on a foggy night. My gymnastics team had just finished competing in the Georgia Classic Invitational earlier in the day, and we decided to treat ourselves to a night out. The only hot spot open on a Sunday night at one in the morning was the local Bowl-A-Rama. So all fifteen of us headed for the dimly lit parking lot. Just as we began descending down the stairs, a piercing laugh broke into our conversations. We rushed down the stairs to see what the commotion was about. To our amazement, we found three guys dancing in the parking lot, two were butt naked. We stood there just gasping at

the alarming sight. The two guys spotted us and ran inside. After the stun of what we saw wore off, we proceeded to the minivans and the bowling alley. A few minutes later the guys emerged from their rooms, fully dressed this time, and proceeded to follow us. Because of our coach Kathie's scenic route driving, we managed to lose them in the old back roads. We finished off the night by bowling for two hours, making fools of ourselves the whole time. When we got back to the motel, there was no sign that the guys were even there, except for a pink shirt, which laid still on the wet pavement.

The coach Sara mentioned in her essay was Kathie Klages, who went on to become the head coach of the gymnastics team at Michigan State.

Sara's star was rising. She often trained with John's select group of top gymnasts—the girls who got the majority of his time and attention at the gym. At the same time, the pressure was mounting. One time when she flubbed on the vault at a competition, John was furious, she recalls. "He picked up the springboard and threw it at me. I felt it hit my leg from behind. This was like a forty- or fifty-pound plank. I stumbled and fell forward, with my leg bleeding," she says. "He said, 'Oh, it must have slipped.'" She tried to brush it off. She knew she was on the verge of joining his top posse for good. This was her dream—and her nightmare. She feared him as much as she craved his approval.

And then, at twelve years old, she crashed.

She suffered an injury so extreme, she could not possibly hide it from the coaches. It happened while she was doing a dismount from a balance beam—a cartwheel at the end of the beam followed by a jump off backward. The beam was elevated on a platform, with a pit of foam blocks below. As she jumped from the beam after the cartwheel, she felt her body twisting in a way that it should not.

"You fall a lot in gymnastics, so you become aware of your body and how to position it so you won't get injured," she says. But in that moment, she didn't think she needed to readjust herself. "I thought I would be fine because I'd be landing in the foam pit."

She was the opposite of fine. She landed on her backside with such force that her feet flew up over the front of her head and her chin smashed into her sternum—actually breaking the bone. She didn't know she had broken anything at the time. She just knew that the shock and pain were so great, she could hardly move. Still, she tried to pull herself up out of the pit to get back on the balance beam. "I didn't want to get in trouble," she says. "I knew I would be blamed." John would be mad. She had to buck up.

As she tried to hoist herself out of the pit, she hoped no one would notice that she was moving in slow motion. "It was like trying to pull myself up out of a swimming pool," she says. It felt more like quicksand. John noticed and asked what was taking her so long. "I said I was hurt; he said I was lying and to get up and do it again," she says. Adding to the horror, she says, "I could feel my whole rib cage moving around in my chest. I could barely breathe. I couldn't take a regular breath, only super-short, shallow ones." That's because breathing made her lungs expand, which made her rib cage move. Still, she tried get back up on that beam. She collapsed instead.

John's wife, Kathryn, drove her to the hospital. Sara tried to stay still, to avoid being jostled amid the searing pain. "Even the smallest movement was painful," she recalls. In the emergency room, she learned the terrible news: her sternum had been broken in two places. John came to visit after practice that night; she remembers only that he looked pale and that she felt gutted. She thought it was all her fault. Three long days in the hospital followed. The doctors wrapped her chest and said her bones would eventually grow back together, but it would take time.

Everything hurt. She couldn't move her shoulders. Bending over felt like torture. One day before she left the hospital, she tried to put her pants on and passed out from the pain. Back at home, she lay in her bed for weeks, unable to sit up on her own. When she finally returned to school, people looked at her as if they were afraid she would break. "In the halls, the teachers were terrified that kids would bump me," she says. "I had to go to class early so I could have the halls to myself." Lunch was solo too: "I ate lunch in the principal's office, not the cafeteria." All the while, she was thinking, When can I get back to the gym?

It took six months. "When the doctor cleared me, I was so happy," she says. "I couldn't wait to get back."

Her parents thought she should quit. "You don't have to keep going," her mom said. But Sara convinced her family to let her continue. She had invested years in the sport; she didn't want to give up now.

"I went running back to the gym and told John, 'My doctor cleared me!'" she says, her eyes misting at the thought of it. Then she cautioned him, "But the doctor said I need to take it easy at first."

This did not compute with John. His reply, she says, shook her: "No you don't." He went on to rant that "doctors don't know what they're talking about; they don't know anything about gymnastics," she recalls. "Those were his exact words."

Astoundingly, during her first day back at the gym after breaking her sternum, she was expected to start where she had left off. John didn't go easy on her, sending her to practice on the vault and bars. She fell on her back, on her hands; everything felt out of whack. John noticed. When she landed on her hands and knees after a vault, he came and sat on her back, pinning her down, she recalls. "He was sitting on my back, riding me in a sexual way," she says. "He said, 'Ooh, baby, you like it like that!' He wanted to humiliate me because I didn't land on my feet." All this, while she tried to come back from a major injury.

Her body had changed during her time off—in many ways. For one, she had grown more than an inch. In addition, her upper body strength had weakened due to the injury. Most alarming, her sternum had grown back together crooked and overlapping, causing constant pain in both her chest and back. "My body felt broken. I felt like I had to learn everything all over again," she says. "Everything hurt so much." Still, she would not think of walking away. "You're conditioned not to quit. That's drilled into your head. You're told to be tough, be strong," she says. "And I loved the rush of gymnastics," she adds. "I'm kind of an adrenaline junkie. You get addicted to it. Nailing those tricks, it's a rush."

She tried valiantly to get back to form, but it wasn't happening quickly, and she felt lost. She knew she was fading in John's eyes. "I wasn't on the same trajectory that I once was," she says. "He was disappointed in me. I could feel it." That hurt even more than the physical pain. She begins to get emotional as she tells me this, then checks herself. In fact, when she sees an empathetic look on my face, she asks that I please not express any sympathy as she recounts her story, because it makes it harder for her; she doesn't want to get upset. I realize that it's all part of the boot camp she grew up in—no crying. I try to refrain from reacting to the wrenching things she is telling me.

She continues her tale, telling me she became even more driven to get John's approval. She had climbed so high at the gym before the injury knocked her down. She refused to let it all slip away. "It had been within reach," she says. "I wanted it back."

John, meanwhile, was gaining in national prominence. He had a number of Level 10 gymnasts now—the highest level in the Junior Olympics, the competitive program run by USA Gymnastics, the governing body for the sport. He wanted Olympians. Sara recalls that he brought in a sports psychologist from Michigan State to help the girls learn to focus at competitions, to block out sounds and distractions around them, to win.

And then one day, Larry Nassar walked in the door.

Chapter Two

The Town

On a recent afternoon in downtown Lansing, Michigan, where Sara began her boot camp all those years ago, an Elvis song fills the air.

"Everybody in the whole cell block . . .
Was dancin' to the Jailhouse Rock."

The music follows you everywhere you go. That's because it's drifting from little speakers on the streetlights. There's a mix of cheery tunes: "Stayin' Alive" by the BeeGees, "Uptown Girl" by Billy Joel. The sidewalks are otherwise fairly quiet on a Tuesday afternoon, like so many main streets across America. A guy bites a slice of pizza while leaning against a pole. There's an old-fashioned clothing department store, a liquor shop, a jewelry repair place, all looking rather empty. A bearded man sitting on the sidewalk asks, "Can you help a veteran?" Three tall smokestacks from a power plant loom in the distance. A train blows its horn from somewhere. A few blocks down, a television reporter interviews a woman in the shadow of the state capitol, its towering dome poking the sky.

In the window of a sports bar, a banner is emblazoned with a giant Spartan head and the words "Go Green, Go White." This is

Michigan State territory, a classic college town. Here, it seems, nearly everyone has a tie to the university: either they know a student or professor, or they're a graduate of the school, or they're a fan of the Big Ten football team. The college has long been a tremendous point of pride for this close-knit community. Until Larry Nassar shook it to its core.

The scandal burst into the news in the fall of 2016, after the *Indianapolis Star* published a sweeping exposé on USA Gymnastics, reporting that the organization, which is based in Indianapolis, had mishandled allegations of sexual abuse at the hands of coaches. When the story came out, Rachael Denhollander, a former gymnast, emailed the newspaper and named Larry Nassar as an abuser. At the time, he was a renowned doctor and professor of osteopathic medicine at Michigan State University, as well as a National Team doctor for USA Gymnastics, where he was famous for treating Olympic athletes. Soon after, two more people called the paper, also accusing the doctor. One was John Manly, an attorney representing gymnast Jamie Dantzscher, who won a bronze medal with her team at the 2000 Olympics.[1] The other was Jessica Howard, a three-time national champion gymnast and member of the USA Gymnastics Hall of Fame.

Jessica shared with me a recording of the voicemail she left for the newspaper: "I just wanted to call you as a follow-up to your story about the USA Gymnastics cover-up of sexual abuse," she said, her voice soft but determined. "I have some information for you, and I am very nervous about talking to you about it, but I think it would help bring justice to a lot of the people who have been affected by USA Gymnastics and their policies."

Jessica wished to remain anonymous at the time, as did Jamie, but their stories provided important backup to the allegations from Rachael, who was ready to publicly identify herself as a survivor. The *Star* ran an article and a video interview with Rachael, and in the months that followed, dozens more women came forward.

To be sure, many women and girls had reported Larry Nassar over the decades—to coaches, counselors, even the police—but they were dismissed or disbelieved. If anyone had listened and believed, this predator could have been stopped much sooner. Hundreds of girls could have been spared.

This time, the police took action. In November 2016, Michigan attorney general Bill Schuette announced a first round of charges of criminal sexual conduct, noting that this was just the "tip of the iceberg." A month later, federal law enforcement officials indicted the doctor for possessing some thirty-seven thousand images of child pornography on his computers. Two months after that came a second round of charges of criminal sexual conduct in Michigan. Women kept coming forward.

In July 2017, Larry Nassar pleaded guilty in federal court to child pornography charges; four months later, he pleaded guilty in two Michigan counties to criminal sexual conduct. He had been abusing young women and girls for nearly three decades, touching their breasts and buttocks and penetrating them vaginally or anally with his hands, without using gloves or medical lubricant. He claimed it was medical treatment. Experts disagreed, noting that while there is an internal treatment that can be used for conditions such as infertility or pelvic pain, it is by no means a common treatment for the kinds of sports injuries he treated. And such a sensitive treatment would require the doctor to get parental consent for minors, to use gloves, to clearly explain the procedure, and to have an assistant in the room—protocols he did not follow.

In December 2017, the doctor was sentenced to sixty years in federal prison for possessing child pornography—images so disturbing, they were "like none other that I've seen," said Judge Janet T. Neff during the sentencing. She slammed him for violating the most basic tenet of medicine: "Do no harm."

And then, a historic courtroom phenomenon grabbed the attention of the world.

In January 2018, more than two hundred women stood up and confronted Larry Nassar in person, one by one, giving a blistering series of victim impact statements at his sentencing hearings in two Michigan counties. Many of the women had been anonymous up to this point, but as more and more women stood up and publicly identified themselves, others drew courage and took the stand too, getting the final say with their betrayer. The nation took notice as the women's faces and words appeared across the news. The women made the case personal. They gave the story a face—more than two hundred faces. They took back the power.

"Perhaps you've figured it out by now, but little girls don't stay little forever," said Kyle Stephens, the first woman to confront the doctor in court. "They grow into strong women that return to destroy your world."

Addressing all of the women who spoke, Judge Rosemarie Aquilina said, "You are no longer victims—you're survivors."

Then the judge tore into Larry Nassar, sentencing him to 40–175 years in prison and telling him, "I just signed your death warrant."

In another courtroom twist, the trailblazing judge read aloud parts of a letter the doctor had written to her during the hearings. Complaining that he was being treated unfairly, he insisted that his methods were "medical, not sexual" and that he had pleaded guilty only to spare the community and his family from the stress of a trial. He said he was a "good doctor" and that "the media" convinced his patients that "everything I did was wrong and bad. They feel I broke their trust. Hell hath no fury like a woman scorned."

When the judge read that last line, the courtroom groaned.

Judge Aquilina later told me, "His letter told me he has no real remorse. Defendant Nassar still believes what he did was medical treatment, and he still desires to control all those around him."

He is now behind bars, where he will remain for the rest of his life.

As of this writing, dozens of officials have been ousted or charged with crimes. At Michigan State, president Lou Anna K. Simon is out, along with the dean of the College of Osteopathic Medicine, Dr. William Strampel, and gymnastics coach Kathie Klages. All three face criminal charges that I will detail later in this book. All have pleaded not guilty. John Engler, an interim president of the university, is also out, along with general counsel Bob Young. Scott Blackmun, chief executive of the US Olympic Committee, and Steve Penny, president of USA Gymnastics, are gone, with Penny facing criminal charges that I will describe later as well. He has pleaded not guilty. Congress is probing all three institutions.

The Department of Justice is reportedly investigating the FBI for sidelining the case.[2] At press time for this book, John Geddert is under investigation by the Michigan attorney general amid complaints of abusive coaching and has been suspended by USA Gymnastics and the US Center for SafeSport, a watchdog group tasked with combating abuse in sports. The Karolyi Ranch, the training center for the US National Team and US Olympic Team, has closed its doors in Texas and is being investigated by law enforcement. The US Olympic Committee has taken steps to decertify USA Gymnastics as the governing body for the sport. Lawsuits have been filed against USA Gymnastics, the US Olympic Committee, John Geddert and his gymnastics club, and others.

Still, there's a long way to go to change the culture of the sport and the institutions that enabled the abuse, the survivors say, in a voice that grows ever louder.

I'm here in Lansing to tell the story of how Larry Nassar infiltrated this community, hunting its girls for nearly thirty years. I'm here to tell the personal stories, the stories behind the headlines, to reveal how he charmed and conned this town into trusting him. How he grew so bold, he abused girls while their unknowing parents were right there in the room, sometimes in his own basement.

This is a story of families broken, a town ripped apart, moments missed when the doctor could have been stopped, and the cynical refining of his method, as seen through the eyes of his targets. It is also a story of tremendous courage and strength, as hundreds of women and girls joined together to bring him down, despite his longtime support from the most powerful institutions in the sport.

It is a narrative spanning decades, from the first known survivor to the last. Across the years, we will meet dozens of courageous women, each with unique insight, including Lindsey Lemke, sisters Izzy and Ireland Hutchins, Autumn Blaney, and Emma Ann Miller, as well as their parents, who tell astonishing untold stories of how the doctor evolved. Many are sharing the details of their lives for the first time in this book, like Sara Teristi, who unveils that the abuse went further than anyone knows. We'll meet Shelby Root, who is also telling her story for the first time. Her story is different than those of the Nassar survivors, but it provides important insight into the Nassar saga, showing how the gymnastics world can damage girls on many different levels. Shelby tells me that John Geddert coached and groomed her for two years and then, when she was eighteen, initiated a sexual relationship when she left his gym in preparation for college—resulting in devastating consequences. We'll meet women who reported the Nassar abuse to the police and to officials at Michigan State, including Larissa Boyce, Brianne Randall-Gay, and Amanda Thomashow, only to be dismissed. We'll get to know national champion Jessica Howard, who served on the board of USA Gymnastics and saw its failings from the inside. And hometown attorney James "Jamie" White, who wrote key legislation with state lawmakers, allowing more time for sex abuse victims to take legal action—crucial for the Nassar case. Plus, fiery Judge Rosemarie Aquilina, who gave the women a powerful voice in court, changing the definition of justice.

The road for the people of Lansing has been rough. "Michigan State is the identity of our community. To have it associated with something so dark was really hard for people," says attorney Jamie White, who has two degrees from Michigan State himself. "But at the end of the day, if we come out of this a stronger and safer place, there's some sun at the end of the rainbow." Jamie ended up playing a remarkable role in the Nassar case, not only representing survivors and writing key legislation, but also becoming a pivotal figure in the financial chess match with his alma mater, using an extraordinary legal strategy to help broker a $500 million settlement—the biggest financial settlement of its kind ever in the United States.

*****

Standing on a Lansing street corner as the sun begins to fade on a recent afternoon, I hear a guy call to me from his pickup: "Hey, where'd you get that hat?" It's just a simple black cap, bought for a beach walk on vacation a few years back. I tell him that I got it from pretty far away, in France. He laughs and motors on. Lansing has a small-town vibe that I know well, having grown up in a much smaller town in southern Indiana. There, my parents published the local newspaper, and we lived along a country road, across from a cornfield and a creek—or a "crick," as people liked to call it. As a kid, I did gymnastics at a Girls Club in a neighboring town. I mastered an aerial cartwheel—no hands—and a back walkover on the balance beam.

I remember how great it felt to nail that aerial cartwheel. I had practiced it in the front yard of our home in the woods over and over, starting off by doing a regular cartwheel and then pulling my hands up until I could do it hands-free. Each week, after practice at the club, feeling exhilarated and out of breath, I looked forward to getting a can of grape soda from the vending machine. It was all fun—no pressure, no stress. A far cry from the hardline gyms like the one in Lansing. There were no gyms like that near my town, and there was no gymnastics team at my school. If there had been such a gym or a team, I would have been there. I would have wanted to keep going too.

I can picture how so many young girls caught the gymnastics bug, wanting to learn and grow.

Some five hundred women have now come forward against Larry Nassar. They rose up and took him down. These are their stories. They are telling them in the hopes of preventing this kind of unthinkable abuse in the future. They call themselves the sister survivors. They are a powerful army in the fight for justice and change.

Sara Teristi is helping to lead that army. She has rare insight into how Larry Nassar morphed into a serial sexual predator. She saw it happen.

Chapter Three

How It Began

On his very first day at Great Lakes Gymnastics, Larry Nassar stood awkwardly as John Geddert introduced him to the young athletes, describing him as a student in medical school at Michigan State. It was late 1988, and Larry had just begun studying osteopathy, a branch of medicine that includes the treatment of health problems through the manipulation of muscles and bones. (Everyone called Larry by his first name, including the girls in his care, and so I am doing the same here.) The girls learned that Larry would be on hand regularly at the gym, volunteering his time to help them with their injuries. John wanted the girls to keep winning.

Sara Teristi's first impression of the new doctor: "He was geeky, nerdy," she says. "He had this *Revenge of the Nerds* laugh, and we all giggled about that." Quite a contrast to the confident, imposing John. "Larry was the complete opposite of suave," she says. "He looked like someone who wanted to fit in with the jocks and never could."

She and I are sitting in the peaceful museum courtyard for a second day, continuing our conversation. It's a few months after the guilty pleas and court hearings, and she is still processing everything. She takes a sip of bottled water and jokes about the metal brace on her knee. The brace is so prominent, she says, that random people can't help but comment, often regaling her with tales of their own injuries. They stop her at the grocery store, the gas station, everywhere, and strike up a conversation. She knows a lot about the injuries of complete strangers, she says with a laugh. I'm impressed that she can find some humor in it. The brace is a constant reminder of the terrible pain she endured as a child from her injuries, the pain she still tries to manage today. Then she takes me back to Larry's early days at Great Lakes Gymnastics.

Larry had some prior experience with the sport. He had begun working with gymnasts as a high school student in 1978, serving as an athletic trainer for the girls' gymnastics team at North Farmington High School in suburban Detroit. In 1981, he earned a high school varsity letter for his work with the team. In 1985, he graduated from the University of Michigan with a degree in kinesiology, the study of the mechanics of body movements. A year later, he began working as an athletic trainer with the US National Team. He described his decades of career moves in a lengthy 2015 Facebook post. The post is no longer visible, but the *Indianapolis Star* got a picture of it before it disappeared and published it.[3]

In 1987, he volunteered at the Pan American Games, and a year later he volunteered at the Olympic Trials, before volunteering for as many as twenty hours a week at Great Lakes Gymnastics, he said in his Facebook post. He had found a strategic way to build his résumé while gaining access to girls—volunteering. Jamie White, the Lansing attorney who would later become a key figure for survivors in the Nassar case, notes, "He actively sought out situations where he could touch little girls all day."

Sara Teristi, who was fourteen in late 1988 when Larry arrived, was still striving for a full comeback from her snapped sternum. But in pushing herself so hard to get past the injury, she risked new injuries, as she would try to avoid putting stress on painful areas of her body while training. One day, while practicing on the uneven bars, she was doing a release move, letting go of the high bar to grab the low bar, when she missed the low bar and wound up slamming into it from behind, smacking her back, hard. A fiery pain shot through her upper body. Fearing John's ire, she told herself, Don't cry. Don't cry. When he found out, John was indeed mad. "First he kicked a bucket," she recalls. "Then he yelled, 'Go see Larry!'"

In a back room of the gym, Larry examined Sara, concluding that the force of the bar against her back had dislocated several ribs. Then he iced her chest and sent her back out to tell John that she was injured. When she did so, she recalls, John said, "So?"

Sara continued training. She didn't take time off, didn't go to the hospital. She did not dare complain. Years later, she learned that at least one of the ribs had actually been broken at the time, meaning she was training with a broken bone without knowing it. "You develop a high threshold for pain," she explains, when I can't help but express alarm. "You go to a place where you can block stuff out. You stop feeling; you stop all emotion. I was like a zombie." Still, she was only human. A few days after injuring her ribs, she tried to bench press, but couldn't lift the bar all the way and let it slam down. "John got mad and asked what was wrong. I told him it hurt, then he said, 'If you're gonna be that much of a wimp, then get out of my gym!' So I sucked it up and finished my sets," she says. "It hurt like hell, but I didn't cry." Her eyes start to water at the memory of it, and again she stops herself. She left for the day, crushed that John had told her to get out, but she came back the next week.

She began seeing Larry regularly. He would massage her chest with ice that had been frozen into little Dixie cups. At first, he left her leotard in place for this process. But soon, he began moving her leotard down. First he moved the straps down over her shoulders. Then he moved her bra straps down. Later he pushed the leotard and bra down low on her chest, until her nipples were exposed. Today, Sara believes he was testing to see how much he could get away with. At the time, she thought he must have a reason for doing what he did, because he was supposed to be a doctor.

Larry, feeling emboldened, went a step further. "I remember the first time he touched my nipples," she says. "Usually, after he iced my chest, he would dab away any excess water with a paper towel. But this time he took the paper towel and wiped my nipples, even though they weren't wet. I thought, Why is he doing that—I'm not wet there. Then I felt his finger touch my nipples. He massaged them and pinched them." She didn't question him. She was a kid, and he was the doctor. Like so many children, she had been taught to trust her doctor. And her morale was at an extreme low at this point. She felt completely discarded by her coach. "I felt like just another body in the gym to him," she says. "I didn't matter to him anymore. He barely talked to me, except to weigh me." And so, as Larry pinched her nipples, she says, "I just lay there, frozen."

What happened next was baffling. Larry suddenly got angry, she recalls, and ordered her to leave the room. "He said, 'You have to ice your own chest from now on.'" Sara didn't know what sparked the wild mood swing. "I was so confused," she says, "I thought I had done something wrong. I thought it must be my fault."

She wonders now if he panicked after going too far with her. Perhaps he pulled back to compose himself after losing control.

After that strange day, she didn't see him for a couple of weeks. Then one day, he invited her back. "This time, he undressed me right away and went straight for my nipples," she says. "He didn't waste any time. He wasn't testing the waters anymore." Again she forced her mind to go blank during the abuse. She felt uncomfortable but still believed in him because he was a doctor, an authority, and she was a kid. It didn't occur to her to say anything to anyone about it. Anyway, she couldn't make any waves or cause any more trouble for herself with John. She needed to get back in his good graces.

The "treatment" continued. Sometimes, she recalls, John would walk into the room when Larry was icing her chest and touching her nipples. "They would stand there and have a conversation right in front of me," she says. She felt embarrassed, lying on her back, topless, while the men chatted. "John would joke about how small my 'tits' were," she says. "He said if I was lucky, they would get bigger." But she wasn't surprised by much of anything at this point. After all, John walked in on the girls in the bathroom, she says. No boundaries, no privacy. In fact, Sara believes John helped set her up for the abuse from Larry, trampling her psyche to a point that she had lost her sense of self. She felt as if her body, her life, were no longer her own. "Your body didn't belong to you," she says. "You didn't get to make decisions about it." She practiced her ability to go numb and block it all out.

If only John had reported Larry's behavior with Sara to authorities, she says, decades of abuse might have been stopped.

Larry's ice "treatment" was not controlling the pain, and her mother pressed her constantly to quit. "I told her there was no way she could make me," Sara says. Even though the sport was taking a brutal emotional and physical toll, the thought of leaving was the worst thing Sara could imagine. She had worked too hard to give up. Gymnastics was her world, her life. She never wanted to regret quitting too soon. So she convinced her mother to let her seek medical help for pain management and keep going. Her mother didn't want to end her daughter's dreams, so she reluctantly agreed. Thus began a parade of different prescriptions from specialists— painkillers, anti-inflammatory drugs, muscle relaxers, steroids. She tried them all, usually one at a time but sometimes in combinations, in addition to popping Advil throughout the day—six of the pills at a time, two or three times a day. "I felt like an old lady with a pill box," she says. "I kept telling myself I could get through it."

The steroids in particular created new problems. For one, they sparked "roid rage," she says, and she took out her frustrations on a school locker one day, ripping the door from its hinges, which prompted a visit to the principal. The steroids also made her gain weight, getting her in trouble at the weigh-ins at the gym. She was five-foot-four and barely one hundred pounds, but she was put on a diet for being overweight. "I was allowed twelve hundred calories a day, while practicing four and a half or more hours a day," she says. "I had to record everything I ate." She remembers being surprised, at a meet in Seattle, to see other coaches letting their gymnasts eat candy bars. She began to desperately seek ways to lose the weight, which soon sent her spiraling. First she tried Slim-Fast powder—hiding it in her closet and eating it dry, straight from the can, in her bedroom so her mom wouldn't see—and skipping meals when she could. When that didn't do the trick, she began secretly spitting food into her napkin at dinner. Sometimes, when she did eat, she made herself throw up, using syrup of ipecac, the medicine used to cause vomiting after poisoning.

Larry began a new treatment with Sara, kneading her bare back, down to her rear, which was partially exposed, making her feel self-conscious. "He would take his forearm and run it up and down my back," she says. The procedure was painful, and, at one point, tears rolled down her face. When he asked what was wrong, she told him, "You're hurting me." She thought he would immediately stop. He did not. "He took his elbow and ground it into my back even harder," she says. She pauses and tells me that she finds it interesting that so many of his more recent victims have described him as a nice guy. He was not nice to her. At one point, she recalls, he admonished her for taking up too much of his time, even though he was the one scheduling the appointments—usually two a day. He had not yet developed the skill to befriend his targets. It is an ability he would hone in the years to come, learning to groom young girls as well as their parents and the community. Sara believes that with her in those early days, he was always testing, learning, figuring out how far he could push it with his young patients. It's what predators do, experts say, gradually testing a child, for instance, by placing a hand on her shoulder or leg or making an inappropriate comment, then escalating if the child doesn't object.

Around this time, Sara witnessed what she believes was a defining moment for Larry Nassar—setting him on his predatory path for years to come.

She saw the incident one day during practice. A gymnast had been injured, and Larry told John that the girl should take a week off. "John got pissed and started throwing things," Sara says. "I remember Larry watching. And then, slowly, very methodically, he changed his mind and said, 'Actually, she doesn't need a week off.'" John's demeanor changed; he stopped raging. He asked Larry if he was sure. The answer: yes. The girl continued training, injured. Sara thinks Larry realized that the way to keep his access to the girls was to please John. And the way to please John was to clear the girls to train and compete when they were injured. "After that, Larry went along with whatever John wanted," Sara says.

The two men would work together for nearly three decades, including at the 2012 Olympics, where they served as team coach and doctor.

Sara, feeling increasingly worthless in the eyes of her coach, entered a dark new realm: she began cutting herself. "When you're in pain twenty-four-seven, and you're being told that you're not in pain—that you're faking it, you're lying—you begin to wonder if it's all in your head," she says. "So I started to cut myself. I wanted to compare the pain from the cuts to the pain from my injuries, to see what was real." In her bedroom, which was now plastered with posters of famous gymnasts, she cut little slits on her hands with a kitchen knife. She jabbed herself with needles and pins. She ripped at her cuticles till they stung. She kept the marks hidden.

Her music tastes grew darker too. Now she preferred heavy metal bands like Metallica to her former, bouncier favorites: Salt-N-Pepa, Paula Abdul, INXS. All the while, she kept trying to impress John. One day, she recalls, she wanted to show him that she had nailed a challenging skill: a front layout with one and a half twists. As she set out to do the flip, he turned away instead of watching her perform. The darkness kept closing in.

In 1990, John became the chair of the Junior Olympic program, according to his LinkedIn page. He was moving up in the gymnastics world. In a testament to her incredible drive, Sara, who was fifteen at the time, had managed to become a Level 9 gymnast, just a rung below the highest level in the Junior Olympic realm, despite her injuries. She had also developed a new injury: a hairline fracture in her tailbone from repetitive stress. One of her coaches helped her get it diagnosed, sending Sara to her chiropractor. But the coach advised Sara not to tell John about the injury, saying, "It will only make things worse for you." The coach was trying to protect her, Sara says, but the idea that she should protect herself by hiding an injury from the head coach was clearly misguided. Nonetheless, she felt she had no choice but to follow the advice.

Meanwhile, the fractured tailbone presented a new opportunity for Larry.

Sara has a difficult time discussing what happened next. At first, she's not sure she wants to tell the whole world. She fears that her boys could get bullied if the kids at school find out about their mom's experience. A few weeks later, thanks in large part to the camaraderie and support she has gained from her fellow survivors, she tells me she is no longer worried about going public with the story and that she thinks it's important to do so. She remembers lying facedown on the table in the back room of the gym, gripping the sides of the table in pain during a procedure, wanting it to be over. Larry was penetrating her anally with his hands, without using gloves or medical lubricant. She recalls a musty smell in the room at times; she later realized it was likely his ejaculating at some point during the procedure while she lay there.

On the days when she smelled the musty odor, he would get mad at her and tell her to get out of the room, she recalls. At the time, she found this mystifying because ordinarily he would help her get dressed after the treatments. She didn't understand what was going on; she was a sheltered young athlete, mired in training. Sexual abuse wasn't on her radar. And neither was sex. She had never dated boys; there was no time for that, what with the demands of training and schoolwork. She hadn't even started her period yet due to all the grueling exercise and low body weight. She knew only that the procedure was excruciating and that it felt endless, and she couldn't wait for it to stop.

She didn't tell anyone because she trusted that her doctor was performing a medical treatment.

It's a typical response, experts say: kids trust the doctor, and they often don't know if they're being abused by a trusted adult. Even if they do sense that something is off, they might feel embarrassed, ashamed, or that they are somehow to blame. Their young brains are still developing throughout their teen years. And who hasn't felt intimidated by a doctor? There's a power imbalance in a doctor's office: the physician is in command; the patient is vulnerable. Girls in gymnastics are especially susceptible to manipulation by adults because they're isolated from their peers from such a young age, forgoing social activities to make time for training. They live in a bubble. When coaches bark at them, the girls fall in line. In addition, boundaries get blurred, because sometimes male coaches *do* legitimately need to grab girls to prevent falls.

In the Nassar case, many of the kids didn't understand that they were being abused. They were children, and he was the doctor—a highly regarded doctor. They thought he was performing a medical procedure. Many didn't tell because they didn't know.

And pain is just part of the deal. "Gymnastics is about bearing it," says Sara. "You're not allowed to have emotions, to complain."

She continued to train with her fractured tailbone and to deal with Larry's "treatments." She didn't think things could get any worse. She was wrong.

Chapter Four

The Coach

While John Geddert was breaking Sara Teristi's spirit, he was breaking another young gymnast's heart.

Shelby Root says he carefully groomed her as her coach at Great Lakes Gymnastics, eventually starting a sexual relationship when she left the gym to prepare for college. Eighteen years old at the time, she was of legal age, but like most gymnasts who grew up embroiled in training, she had no experience with dating or sex. And this man—eleven years her senior—had been her coach, a person she had been taught to trust and obey. A vulnerable teen, she became entangled with him, thinking he loved her, she says, but he would later discard her, leaving her feeling abandoned and suicidal.

Her story is different from those of the Nassar survivors, but it reveals a very important layer in the long-running Nassar saga. It shows how the world of gymnastics—in which doctors and coaches have the inherent trust of young girls and their parents—can create an environment that enables grooming on many different levels, leading to serious fallout.

It wasn't an easy decision for Shelby to share her story in these pages. She knew it would be stressful to put herself in the public eye and reopen old wounds. "I feel it is my responsibility," she says, speaking to me by phone from Australia, where she now lives. She wants to help young girls and their parents recognize the grooming process and avoid an emotionally damaging situation that can ripple across a lifetime, as it did for Shelby.

I sought comment from John Geddert, via his attorneys, but did not receive a reply. I also contacted the US Center for SafeSport, the watchdog group that suspended him after the Nassar scandal amid complaints of abusive coaching. An official pointed out a pertinent tenet in the group's code of conduct: "Once a coach-athlete relationship is established, a power imbalance is presumed to exist throughout the coach-athlete relationship, regardless of age, and is presumed to continue for minor athletes after the coach-athlete relationship terminates, until the athlete reaches twenty years of age."

Shelby first met John when she began training at Great Lakes Gymnastics in 1985. A sixteen-year-old who wore her golden-brown hair in barrettes, she had just learned how to drive in her parents' dark-blue Monte Carlo. She sported three piercings in one ear and one in the other and embraced the eighties trend of wearing her charcoal stirrup pants with a pink V-neck sweater—which she wore backward with the V in back. She liked the TV show *Remington Steele*, starring Pierce Brosnan as a debonair thief turned detective. She typed her school papers on a typewriter and talked on a rotary dial phone in the family kitchen, with listening ears all around.

She had transferred to Great Lakes Gymnastics from a smaller club, eager to learn. Sara Teristi, meanwhile, was in her early days at the gym as well, having joined during the prior year at age ten.

Shelby was in top physical shape but needed to sharpen her technical skills. Wearing her favorite leotard—black, white, and yellow, with flowers at the top and stripes across the waist—she quickly excelled, and John noticed. He began asking her to come to the gym early, before afternoon practice, she says. He would help her develop her skills during that time, coaching her one-on-one before the other girls arrived. While he did sometimes bark at her during practice, he didn't target her as much as some of the other gymnasts, especially those who got injured. With Shelby, he took the time to talk with her, about school, family, life. "He paid attention to me. He would sit and talk and listen. It felt good to have someone so interested in me—an adult, someone I respected. It was a vulnerable time for me. I was feeling pretty disconnected from my parents at home; my sister was away at college," she says. "That's how it started."

Looking back, she says, "I can see that John was grooming me; he was taking small, gradual steps. It was subtle. Just as a coach helps you build up all the skills to do a new trick, he took the same approach with me, building up my friendship and trust. He was very patient, very methodical. But when you're young, and you're working with a coach of his caliber, it doesn't occur to you that he doesn't have your best interests at heart," she says. "You trust the coach implicitly." She notes that he was still finding his footing as a coach in those early years as well: "When he was coaching me, he wasn't the overly confident figure that he is today." But she could sense his ambition. "He seemed like he had something to prove." Larry, meanwhile, had not yet started volunteering at the gym.

Shelby's skills were dramatically improving, and John was clearly pleased with her progress. "He said, 'I think you might have a chance at a college scholarship.' He believed in me when no one else did," she says. "I needed that, and he saw it." He kept inching closer, hugging her when she did well at meets. "You can communicate a lot in a hug. Sometimes they lasted a bit too long or were tighter. I could tell when he was happy with me."

Her longtime best friend, Dr. Seann Willson, an orthopedic surgeon and former gymnast at Great Lakes Gymnastics, recalls, "She was a lost high school girl with little support and misunderstood at home. She worked hard, became a great gymnast, and he gave her attention, a lot of attention. Attention she so desperately needed. He clearly groomed her. He was good at it."

Shelby ended up getting a full-ride athletic scholarship to the University of Iowa. When she graduated from high school in 1986, John attended her graduation party, she says, giving her a necklace with a gold charm engraved with the letter S. By this point, John had gained the trust of her parents as well. They had seen him help Shelby improve her skills and get a college scholarship; they thought he was great. "Like me, they believed he cared for me and only had my best interests in mind," Shelby says. "He gave them no reason to question his trust or his intentions."

The summer after her high school graduation, she was seventeen years old, a fan of the bands Boston and Bon Jovi, as well as the Robert Palmer video "Addicted to Love" on MTV. John invited her to travel to a competition in Florida, along with one of her teammates and a couple of other coaches. Shelby wasn't competing at this meet because she hadn't qualified; her season was over, and John was no longer coaching her, but he said she could come along and support her teammate, and so she did. At the end of the competition, the group sat around an outdoor bar by the beach, and the coaches bought the girls fruity cocktails. Shelby, having grown up in gymnastics with no social life or dating experience, had never tried alcohol, and of course, she was not legally old enough to drink. It didn't take long for her to feel woozy.

Later that night, John strolled down the beach with her. "He walked me out to the water. He put his arms around my waist," she says. "He was holding me. He said, 'I don't know what I'm going to do without you.' I remember thinking I didn't know what I would do without him either." It was another little test from him. She didn't pull away. He took note.

Later that summer, John invited her to attend another meet with him, again saying she could come along to support a teammate. On that trip, which she believes was in Ohio, John built on the romantic moment from the beach in Florida and made a much bolder move, she says, taking advantage of his sway over her as her former coach. "It was a safe time for him to try it. I was eighteen, getting ready to go off to college." She and John were swimming in the hotel pool one night, along with another coach and Shelby's teammate, and eventually the others left and went to bed, leaving just Shelby and John. He flirted with her in a playful way, she says, splashing her and grabbing her legs under the water.

"I remember he eventually had me with my back against the pool wall, and he was in front of me, one arm on each side, and he kissed me for the first time. I remember being surprised and not sure how to react, and I went along with it," she says. Then he escalated. "He moved my bathing suit bottom over to the side and proceeded to have sex with me. It was my first time, so I didn't have any experience and wasn't sure how to respond." She didn't worry about being seen because she trusted him as her former coach, assuming that everything "must be all right," she says. "I didn't have protection, nor did he. I didn't think or consider any consequences. I followed his lead, didn't question, and trusted. I did what I had been trained to do." She adds, "I remember being confused that he picked me. There wasn't anything special about me. I had just gotten my braces off earlier that year. I was just an average girl."

Shelby went back to her hotel room afterward, alone, feeling numb. "I remember thinking, I guess I just had sex," she says. "I thought, I'll never have my first time again." She didn't allow herself to feel emotional about it. "Gymnasts are taught to set aside emotion, anxiety," she says. "That's the only way you stay on the beam." At the same time, she was a romantic. She loved the book *Gone with the Wind* and its heroine, Scarlett O'Hara.

That fall, she headed to college in Iowa and stayed in touch with John. "My phone bill was huge," she says. These were the days of whopping long-distance charges, before cell phones arrived. John also called, visited, and sent letters—handwritten notes, before the advent of email—and she kept the letters in a big cardboard box, the packaging for her boom box. Over the months, she wanted to be closer to home, and to him. So she transferred to Central Michigan University for her sophomore year in the fall of 1987, with John's help. He had gone to the same school and competed as a gymnast, and he put in a good word with the coach. Shelby got a full-ride scholarship and continued her athletic career on the college team. She also kept seeing John. Throughout her sophomore year, the two continued to send letters back and forth. He also visited her at college, staying overnight in her dorm room or at a hotel, she says. "It was not a secret—everybody knew about us." Sometimes he brought her gifts from his travels to competitions, including a teal-blue oversize shirt from a trip to Europe with "Bella" emblazoned across the front in big black letters. "I was completely, totally, utterly in love with him," she says, noting that he said he had separated from his wife. "He said he wanted to marry me and have kids one day. I thought it was real."

She didn't talk with her parents much about John. She remained rather distant from them during this time, which John knew, she says, and used to his advantage. "I was in love with him, the kind of innocent, naive, and fierce love you only have for your first love. So by the time my parents found out, it was too late."

Shelby's mother, Connie Root, recalls, "I did know of the relationship with John but did not recognize the grooming behaviors. After her eighteenth birthday, I suspected a sexual relationship. The sexual nature was not discussed, but, as a mom, I knew. John went to see Shelby the year she was at the University of Iowa and continued after she transferred to Central Michigan University."

Shelby's belief in John began to unravel when she heard a shattering claim. It came from the boyfriend of a gymnast on her team at Central Michigan. "John's sleeping around," he told her. "He's cheating on you." Shelby called John and asked what was going on, and things quickly went south. Several emotional phone calls followed, with her crying and wondering what was true. She couldn't believe he would betray her in such a way. "He said he would come see me and we could talk about it in person," she says. He never did. "He just stopped coming to visit." To have her first love end so abruptly, without any empathy or emotion on his part, she says, left her feeling devastated and depressed, to the point where she thought about killing herself. "This was easily the darkest my life had ever been." She didn't know how to cope with the shock, sadness, and confusion. She was a teenager, and he was an adult man. She couldn't fathom how he could talk about their future, she says, and then just disappear. "I remember thinking, each day, how am I going to get through this day? I thought it was my fault. You can't overestimate how ashamed I felt, honestly believing with every bone in my body that it was my fault and my responsibility." At the time, she says, she couldn't see the responsibility that John bore.

That wasn't the last Shelby saw of John. During her junior and senior years of college, he showed up at occasional meets where she competed, either at Central Michigan or Michigan State. "You never could be sure when or where he'd decide to show up," she says. He would sit on the bleachers near the front, and she could hear him cheering for her. He acted as if nothing had happened, as if he hadn't talked about their future together, she recalls. While she was still reeling from sadness, he was pretending that everything was fine. More confused by his behavior than ever, she avoided him at the meets. She tried to keep her head, to concentrate on her performance. She used the gymnastics training of her childhood to try to block him out. But it was exceedingly painful, she says. Adding to her anxiety, Central Michigan didn't have year-round training facilities at the time, so during the summer, when school was out, she had to train at Great Lakes Gymnastics and see John every day. Again, he acted as if nothing had happened.

Despite the emotional turmoil, she managed to keep her focus and perform so well at competitions that she eventually got named to the Central Michigan University Athletic Hall of Fame, with coach Jerry Reighard saying in a statement at the time, "Shelby was the gymnast that put Central Michigan University gymnastics on the map. She brought a competitiveness and an attitude of being a champion that hadn't been found yet during my time as coach at CMU. She set a competitive standard here that everyone else could follow."

"I wanted to prove to John that I didn't care," Shelby recalls. "I thought, I'll show you by doing this incredible routine, to show that you don't have any effect on me anymore." But she did care, of course. His betrayal would cast a shadow over her relationships for years to come, making it difficult for her to love and trust anyone, she says. Her friend Seann recalls, "She was devastated when it ended. He was the one who made her dreams come true—college scholarship, first love. She spent decades of guilt, shame, and with an inability to trust herself or others."

Shelby graduated from college and moved to Indianapolis, where she worked at an information technology services company. "I wanted to go where no one knew me and start over," she says. "I struggled to figure out who I was, because 'gymnast' had been my identity for my entire life." She ran into John once in Indianapolis, while she was working at the world championships. She continued to blame herself for the traumatic experience with him, she says, even though he was the trusted former coach, the man in the position of power who initiated sex with a teenage girl. Shelby would eventually come to understand that it was not her fault, but not for a long time to come.

She heard from John again in 2007, when he had found some old photo albums with pictures of her from her travels as a gymnast in her teens. He reminisced about old times and asked how she was doing.

She would hear from John one more time after that—nearly a decade later. He would contact her on Facebook, after the Nassar scandal hit the news. His words, which we'll read later, would floor her.

Chapter Five

Goodbye to All That

As Sara Teristi entered her senior year of high school, in 1991, colleges came calling, seeking to recruit her. She was so very close to her goal of getting that gymnastics scholarship she had imagined all those years ago. At the same time, her injuries were adding up, threatening her dream—and making her more of a target for Larry.

She had torn the cartilage in her knee and developed complications with her ribs, which had never healed properly. The pain in her chest became so severe, in fact, that she had to take a few months off to try to heal. "John had given up on me by that point, so he didn't care if I took the time," she says. In fact, he had taken to taunting her because she had developed a lump on her chest where one of her ribs had reconnected badly. He called the bump her "third boob," Sara says. He joked that her other two breasts needed to catch up to the size of the third.

"You're a kid; you laugh it off. I started calling it my third boob too," she says. "But deep down, it devastated me."

Then he began using "Third Boob" as her nickname, calling her by that name instead of Sara in front of the other girls.

Around this time, Larry began taking Sara and other girls out of the gym for medical studies he claimed he was conducting. Sara remembers going to a medical office and that it looked old and worn, not white and modern; she believes it was at Michigan State. There, he would x-ray the girls' wrists, claiming he was researching growth plates, she recalls. Afterward, she remembers stopping by his apartment with him. When Sara and I first begin talking, she recalls a few memories of the apartment: gymnastics magazines spread out on a coffee table by the sofa in his living room and a small bowl of potpourri atop the toilet in the bathroom. More memories would soon return, unthinkable ones.

*****

Trinea Gonczar was another child gymnast who wound up in Larry's apartment. He had been treating her for minor injuries since his arrival at Great Lakes Gymnastics in 1988, taping her wrists and shins at the gym. He'd taken the time to show her mom how to carefully tape her up, and the family thought he was thoughtful and considerate. Trinea was an eager young athlete like Sara, pushing herself to excel. John Geddert would occasionally yell at her, she tells me, but he didn't target her as much as some of the other gymnasts. "John kind of picked specific people who he was hard on," she says. "I would stick up for my teammates and get in trouble for talking back." Larry began abusing her in 1989 or 1990, she recalls, when she was eight or nine years old, suffering from hip pain after a fall from a horse that bucked when it got stung by a bee while she was horseback riding. She had dislocated her left hip and taken the time to heal, but the hip continued to give her problems, sometimes popping out of joint in practice, particularly when she did moves that required a straddle. Larry suggested that she go to his apartment for an ice bath to reduce the swelling since the gym didn't have a bathtub. Her family thought it was generous of him to invest his time in helping her. He was becoming more than a doctor—a friend, they all thought.

Her mom drove her to Larry's place and sat in a chair and waited while Trinea went to take the cold bath. "Larry filled the tub with ice, and I sat there, with ice up to my waist, staring at an egg timer," she recalls. While waiting about fifteen minutes for the timer to ding, she flipped through a gymnastics magazine. Afterward, she wrapped herself in a towel while Larry filled the tub with warm water. She stepped back into the tub for a few minutes, then dried herself off, put on a T-shirt and shorts, and met Larry in the living room. There, he had her lie facedown on a table. He moved the table while she was on it, angling it so that he could obstruct her mother's view of what he was about to do. Then he massaged her and penetrated her vaginally with his bare hands. "I don't remember him discussing what he was doing," Trinea says. Instead, he casually bantered with her and her mom, as if everything was just fine.

He was already taking his strategy to the next level—having an unknowing parent in the room during the abuse. This made kids feel like everything must be OK, because Mom or Dad was there. It was a tactic he would use time and again with girls in the years to come.

"I had so much trust in him," Trinea says, explaining that since he had fixed her wrists and shins, she naturally assumed he was performing a treatment that would help with her hip. As a child, it never occurred to her that a doctor would harm her. "My grandpa was a surgeon. I was raised that doctors do no harm," she says. She went for many more ice baths at his apartment. She remembers that sometimes, other girls would be leaving as she arrived. Over the next decade, Larry would go on to abuse her more than eight hundred times—at his apartment, at the gym, and, later, at a sports medicine clinic at Michigan State. He would also convince her that he was a friend; he was developing his grooming skills. Once, when she had to have ovarian surgery, she woke up in the recovery room to see Larry there, smiling reassuringly. She attended his wedding in her teens and told him about her backpacking adventures through Europe in her twenties. She thought he was a friend for life. Until one day, in her midthirties, she realized with horror, she never knew him at all, as we will see when we come back to her story.

Sarah Klein was yet another young gymnast who ended up in Larry's apartment, starting in the early nineties. She had been seeing him for injuries and sprains at Great Lakes Gymnastics since 1988, when she was eight years old. "He had this big black medical bag, full of supplies," she tells me, and she thought he seemed nice, "smiley," and socially awkward, like "a big Labrador puppy." At the gym, he began massaging her butt in the back room, with her leotard pulled up, exposing her rear and giving her a "wedgie," she recalls. He said the massage would help with back and hip pain; she trusted him because he was supposed to be the doctor. Like Sara Teristi, she was also struggling to survive John's oppressive coaching style, saying, "We were all in perpetual terror in John's gym. He is personally responsible for why none of us developed a sense of self. We developed no boundaries. He robbed us of our voices before we even got our voices." She adds, "Then you have Larry saying, 'Come here, little girl, I'll help you.'"

When she was twelve years old and the doctor had gained her family's friendship and trust, Sarah went to his apartment alone to participate in a supposed study on flexibility for Michigan State. He told her to undress and take a bath to warm up her muscles, saying it would increase her flexibility. Then, as she lay on his table, he penetrated her with his bare hands, feigning his medical study. He would continue to penetrate her vaginally and anally for years, she says, while pretending to be her close friend, further developing his predatory skills. She would later call his actions "a robbery" when she stood up to confront him in court, after he was finally brought to justice. "Your legacy is that you are quite possibly the greatest perpetrator of sexual abuse of all time," she told him. "That, my former friend and loved one, is yours to live with." Sarah would go on to become a force for survivors, which we'll see later.

*****

Meanwhile, by the time Sara Teristi was a senior in high school, her state of mind was extremely rocky. To show me, she pulls out a spiral notebook—a diary she kept for a class in high school during her senior year, detailing her day-to-day life. Her mother had found it in an old box of gymnastics medals and sent it to her years ago. Sara flips through the notebook, her hand shaking a little as she reads the words, deciding what to share with me. She looks at one of the yellowing pages and her eyes well up. "I can't bear to read this," she says, handing the journal to me.

Handwritten in pencil, in neat, slightly backward slanting penmanship, the diary entries are indeed heartrending. Sara had to show them to her teacher every day for class.

In an entry from September 5, 1991, she wondered if she should quit:

Why do I do it? Why do the pain, pressure, frustration, and agony of practice? I've been doing gymnastics for almost 12 years now and I'm getting tired of it. I practice so much, I don't have time for much else. Going 4 to 5 days a week for 4 1/2 to 5 1/2 hours is a little much. I do enjoy the sport (however lately it hasn't been much fun) most of the time, but trying to work in pain and trying to deal with a not so positive attitude becomes hard.

My rib won't heal. It keeps getting worse even though I've taken almost three months off, and my knee is starting to get worse again. I think I want to quit, but can I really throw away 12 years of my life? I only have one year left, maybe I can handle it, but I really don't know if that's possible. This could just be a phase I'm going through (I've been through them before), but this seems more real. I don't know if I can last until I'm over it. Oh well, enough negative talk, I have to get myself packed up for practice in 2 hours. So I'll think positive and have a good attitude . . .

I'm having a great day.

Practice is fun.

Everything is wonderful.

I can do it.

I love gymnastics.

I love gymnastics.

Now, if only I can make myself believe. I want to believe. Oh, I want to believe. I feel like just going somewhere and screaming my head off and hitting a wall.

In an entry dated September 10, worries about her weight crept in:

Well let's see, what shall I write about? Hmmm? I have to go to practice today. That should be a blast. I sure hope I don't get weighed today. I'm so fat. Okay not way too fat but overweight. Last night I went to Campus Life. That was fun. Afterward I went home and did my homework. Not Fun. It's only Tuesday and it feels like Thursday. I'm so tired. I got up at 6:40 and showered and got ready and was out the door by 7:00. I hate it when I get up late, but lately I can't get myself out of bed. (This is really stupid but I don't know what else to write.)

On September 24, she felt anxious about her doctors:

Well well isn't this special. I have to go to the doctor today. He's so stupid! All we do is fight. He comes and tells me I have to quit gymnastics, and I say yeah right. We usually fight for about 30 minutes. It's so great! NOT!!!!

Well after I go to Blair (the above doctor), I'm going to Dr. Jacobz (this is the ninth doctor I've been to for my stupid rib!). I'm beginning to hate doctors. They know nothing! They just say, stop gymnastics. They don't under-stand. I can't quit. I've been doing gymnastics for 12 years. It's my life! I don't know what I'd do w/o it!

At the bottom of that last entry, her teacher weighed in with an oddly distant note, in red ink: "Sounds like my husband's attitude—he hates doctors too!"

On November 6, Sara lamented the loss of her drug supply:

Yesterday at practice I started doing more stuff. My rib still hurts, but I guess it will never totally go away. My doctor says I don't have to go back anymore unless it starts acting up again. He also cut off my supply of Feldan. I hope it doesn't get worse. That's all I need.

My dad woke me up last night and asked me if I wanted my b-day present early. It's a CD player. Big surprise.

On November 8, a dark and frightening entry:

I really don't think I can write today. I'm too mad! I want to hurt something. I hate school, gymnastics, life! I had this dream last night that I cut my throat and I was sitting in a pool of blood, but the cut kept healing so I cut it again and again but I couldn't die. Maybe it means something.

Her teacher commented on that one too, but again, in a disconnected way, not seeming to recognize a student on the verge of a breakdown: "Pretty gruesome dream you had! It probably has to do with your feelings of anger and frustration. Maybe you feel like you can't act out against what is upsetting you, so you turn the anger against yourself. Just a hypothesis."

Sara scribbled a note in pencil in reply: "You're right. I do that a lot to myself, every day."

Her senior year would be her last in gymnastics.

On the day she said goodbye to John Geddert for good, she drove to the gym in her blue 1978 Oldsmobile Cutlass, crying all the way. "I was trying to figure out if I was doing the right thing, if it really was too much to take anymore," she says. "I felt like I owed my parents. I had trained so hard for so long, and I thought I was being weak, letting everyone down." When she parked the car, the angle of her arms as she turned the steering wheel made her ribs throb in pain, and she knew she'd made the right decision. "I remember sitting in my car, trying to pull myself together. I walked in the gym, fully clothed. It felt weird being in there without a leotard on. I saw John over by the bars, so I walked across the floor, and he saw me and met me halfway." Holding back tears, she told him she was done. His response surprised her.

"He told me it was OK, that I could stay and do whatever I wanted in practice and meets. We had a meet coming up in Hawaii, and he said I could go to that and not compete; I could just go for fun or support. I said no, that wasn't fair to the rest of the girls. He asked if I was sure. I said I was. He said I was welcome back whenever I wanted. He gave me a hug, and I walked off. I said goodbye to a couple of coaches and girls—completely avoiding Larry's room—then went outside to my car and cried hysterically."

Her parents, however, were thrilled; she had finally stopped. But not entirely: she finished out the year on her high school team, which seemed like a breeze compared to Great Lakes Gymnastics.

Sara would puzzle over that mysterious final moment with John for years to come. "I always thought it was strange that John was so willing to let me do anything I wanted, if I would just stay. He was going to let me travel to any meet, just as a spectator, or to compete in only one event—whatever I wanted. I was never allowed to make decisions like that, ever. This was so against everything I had been told for my entire career. There were always negative repercussions if you said you didn't want to do something. So why was he offering this now? Why did he want me to stay so badly? That was not him. He would never allow anyone choices like that," she says. "I wondered what his real motivation was. Did he feel guilty for breaking me, for making me practice so many times when I truly was injured? Was he trying to keep me there for Larry or to keep me quiet about what Larry did to me? I will never know the real reason."

By the time she left John's gym, Larry had escalated his abuse, doing something so unthinkable to Sara in his apartment that she would bury the memory for decades. "You put things away in a box," she says. "Some things are too painful. Your brain tries to protect you; it does what it needs to do." When she and I first met, the memory hadn't come back to her yet. She remembered only that she was in his apartment alone at some point. But the full memory was on its way. Soon it would come slamming to the surface.

In my reporting on sexual abuse over the years, many women have told me similar stories of burying traumatic memories from their childhood. One was Barbara Dorris, a survivor of priest abuse. Barbara, a humanitarian who now works with survivors of clergy abuse, was six years old when her priest called her mother and asked her to send Barbara to the church to help with chores. Her mom told Barbara to put on a nice outfit and go. "My mother told me very specifically to wear my very best dress and my Mary Janes. But I was a tomboy; I hated those stupid shoes," Barbara told me. "So I wore my favorite brown shoes, snuck out the back door of the house, and went to the church." There, her priest betrayed her in the most unthinkable way. "The priest said to me, 'You are an evil child, and I have been sent by God to save your soul.' He raped me, and I assumed the rape was the punishment for disobeying Mom. In a kid's world, that's logical," she said. As a child, Barbara had no words to even describe the ordeal. She told no one. And she kept it from herself too, burying the memory for decades, until another trauma—the sudden death of her father—made it come crashing back. As the memories returned, it dawned on her that throughout her life, the sound of church bells had given her a dark feeling. Now she knew why.

Sara had the same dark feeling when she smelled potpourri throughout her life—the kind of potpourri Larry kept in his bathroom.

The year Sara left Great Lakes Gymnastics, she had a rough time, wrestling with depression and a sense of emptiness at giving up her dream. "It's like a death, when you leave something you've worked so hard for," she says. "The goal is no longer there." She managed to control the eating disorder but continued to cut herself on and off. The pain from her injuries remained, and she needed knee surgery. "I felt like a wimp, a quitter," she says. "I had huge guilt about everything. I blamed myself."

She continues to grapple with feelings of guilt today over the entire childhood ordeal and the fallout. "Honestly, even to this day, I cannot say that I don't blame myself," she says. When she tells me this, I can't help but express some emotion, despite her request that I not. I remind her that she was a child. She knows that blaming herself is irrational. She says she's working on it. "My therapist tells me to talk to the girl inside me," she says. She admits that if she heard someone else telling a story like hers, she would insist: "It's not your fault!" But when it comes to her own life, the brainwashing of her childhood runs deep. In her mind, it is her fault that she broke her sternum and had all those subsequent injuries, causing her gymnastics career, and her life, to spin out of control. She thinks she should have concentrated more, as her coach always said.

Sara went on to attend college at Western Michigan University. During her sophomore year, she had a sexual experience with a guy that sparked a memory of Larry's tailbone treatment. "I thought, Hmm, that's the way Larry touched me," she says. Back in high school, she had assumed the treatment was medical, but suddenly she wondered if it was sexual. Looking back now, she thinks she probably didn't really want to know. At the time, she was living off campus with three college roommates, still emotionally out of balance. She was far from her honor roll days, straining to get through her classes; she often tried to drink away her anxiety. She had still not uncovered the worst memory of Larry's abuse, but it was lurking deep below the surface. Sometimes, she had thoughts of suicide.

She knew she needed help. In 1993, she called a campus suicide hotline, then later called Student Health Services to make an appointment with a free campus therapist. When she met the therapist, Sara began talking about her agonizing years in gymnastics and how the experience haunted her—how she would get in trouble for being injured, the questionable treatment by the doctor. Telling the story made her nervous, and the words came out in a rush. She doesn't remember the therapist's name but recalls that she had dark eyes and sat facing a window, at a desk covered with a mess of folders and papers.

The counselor didn't help Sara sort through her painful experiences. And she didn't ask questions about the potentially abusive doctor. In fact, she stopped listening altogether. She cut Sara off as she was speaking. "She interrupted me to ask if I was embellishing," Sara says. "She said no coach or doctor would be allowed to treat their athletes that way. Basically, she thought I was making it up." In her vulnerable state, Sara felt embarrassed. "I shut up and didn't say anything else. I thought I must be crazy. I just stared as she continued to talk. I couldn't wait to run out of there."

Had her therapist listened, asked a few questions, and gone to authorities, hundreds of girls might have never met Larry Nassar.

Sara wouldn't talk about it again until she had a chilling experience decades later, which we will see when we return to her story.

Chapter Six

The Disbelieved

Throughout the nineties, more young women and girls stepped forward to report the unconventional "treatment" practiced by Larry Nassar, alerting coaches, counselors, athletic trainers. But it didn't deter him. If anything, it gave him more strength because the complaints failed to hinder him. He kept gaining power and prestige, becoming unstoppable.

In 1993, he received his osteopathic medical degree from Michigan State. Interestingly, it almost didn't happen. After his first two semesters, he got kicked out of school for failing biochemistry twice. He wrote about it years later on Facebook, saying that in order to remain in school, he had to plead his case before a panel of doctors and professors.[4] "They explained to me that my priorities were mixed up. I was spending too much time in the gymnastics gym and not enough time studying for medical school," he wrote. He asked for more time to finish school; they said no. So he enlisted the help of his friends in gymnastics, including John Geddert, who wrote a letter on his behalf. Larry returned to medical school on a five-year plan instead of four. He graduated and did his residency at a local hospital while still volunteering at Great Lakes Gymnastics—and targeting more girls.

Chelsey Markham was among the girls who told someone about the abuse.

In 1995, when she was ten years old, Chelsey fell from a balance beam in a gymnastics class in Roseville, Michigan, injuring her back. Her coach recommended that she see Larry, so her mother, Donna Markham, began driving her to Lansing for appointments several times a month. Decades later, in a heartbreaking victim impact statement in court, Donna described how Chelsey was twelve years old when she seemed upset and withdrawn after one of her appointments with Larry. Instead of having a mother-daughter lunch at their favorite café like usual, Chelsea just wanted to go home. They got in the car, and Donna pressed her daughter to tell her what was wrong. Chelsey began sobbing and confided that Larry had been penetrating her with his bare fingers, and it hurt. Donna had been in the room with her during the appointments, but Larry had strategically positioned himself so that she couldn't see.

Donna wanted to confront him immediately. "I said, 'Chelsey, we're going back right now.' I mean, I was literally going to drive across the median on 96," she said in court. But Chelsey begged her not to say anything, for fear it would jeopardize her future in gymnastics. "She was hysterical," Donna said, her face crumpled in pain at the memory. "She said, 'Mom, please don't do that.' I said, 'Why?' She said, 'Because you don't understand. Everybody will know. And everybody will judge. And the judges will know when I compete.'"

Given her daughter's panic, Donna didn't confront the doctor but reported him to the coach the next day. "He said, 'Oh no, that couldn't have happened. I've known Larry for years.'"

If only the coach had listened.

Donna talked to other parents too, but they said they hadn't heard of any abuse. For Chelsey, the years that followed became increasingly cloudy and troubled. "She had this self-loathing. I had her see a psychiatrist, and it didn't seem to be helping. There was a lot of self-blame," Donna said in court. "The worst part for her was that this was a man that was supposed to be the best in his field. He was supposed to help her heal. But he didn't. He abused her. He sexually abused her. And he had the audacity to do that while I was sitting right there in the room."

Tragically, Chelsey couldn't escape the depression over time, and she took her life in 2009. "Every day I miss her. Every day. And it all started with him. It all started with him. It just became worse as the years went by, until she couldn't deal with it anymore," Donna said in court. "It has destroyed our family. I went through four years of intense therapy trying to deal with all this, until I could finally accept the fact that this was not my fault. It was the fault of Larry Nassar that started all this with my daughter."

Following the moving testimony, Judge Rosemarie Aquilina, who offered personal words of encouragement to everyone who spoke in court, thanked Donna for standing up for Chelsey, saying, "Someday you'll be reunited with your beautiful daughter. I am sure she will thank you, but I am sure she's hugging you right now."

I checked in with Donna around a year after her court statement. She told me about another deep emotional layer to her story, describing how her older daughter had blamed her for many years after Chelsey's death, saying she should have done more to help Chelsey. But now her older daughter is a mother herself, and she has come to understand that "mothers do everything they can to protect their children," Donna says. Today, she says, "Our relationship has never been better."

Throughout the nineties, Larry continued to slither to the top. In 1996, he was appointed national medical coordinator for USA Gymnastics.[5] He attended the Olympics in Atlanta, where he appeared in an iconic news photo, extending an outstretched hand to gymnast Kerri Strug as she was carried off the floor, cringing in pain from an injury. The same year, he married his wife, a physician's assistant and athletic trainer. John Geddert was a member of his wedding party.

Around this time, John got fired from Great Lakes Gymnastics, according to the *Lansing State Journal*.[6] He had brought success to the club in the form of wins and scholarships, steering gymnasts to more than fifty state championships, eleven individual championships, and five all-around national championships, according to the *Journal*, but his colleagues had some concerns about his coaching style. A co-owner of the club told the *Journal* that the initial goal of the gym had been to provide "a positive gymnastics environment for everybody. Under John, we found ourselves moving farther and farther away from that idea."

John opened a new gymnastics club with his wife in Dimondale, the small town outside of Lansing, in 1996, according to his LinkedIn page. They called it Gedderts' Twistars USA Gymnastics Club. Larry began volunteering his time at Twistars.

In 1997, Larry got his job as an assistant professor and team doctor at Michigan State University and also as a physician for student athletes at Holt High School.[7] Larry also worked at the Michigan State Sports Medicine Clinic, where he treated not just gymnasts but a wide range of patients—from across the university as well as from the broader Lansing community.

The same year, another young gymnast, Larissa Boyce, came forward to report the abuse.

Larissa was participating in a youth gymnastics program at Michigan State, and she remembers that Larry had a "godlike status," which he used to his advantage. She was sixteen years old, she tells me, when Larry started treating her for lower back pain at the Michigan State clinic. She recalls how he began subtly crossing lines, unhooking her bra without warning and massaging her back. Then he would brush his hands down the sides of her body and touch her nipples. As a young girl, she thought that perhaps he didn't realize how close he was getting to sensitive areas. At each visit, he pushed the boundaries a little more. The first time he penetrated her with his bare hand, "I was in shock," she says. "I didn't know what to think about it."

After that, he kept doing it, sometimes at the field house at the university where the girls practiced. "He would abuse me, and I would go back to practice," she says. "My parents didn't know he was even seeing me there." Feeling increasingly uneasy, she wondered if she should tell someone. "I worried, If I say something, will I be believed? I thought, What if I just have a dirty mind?" One day in her backyard, while jumping on the trampoline with a younger gymnast, Larissa summoned the guts to ask her friend what she thought of the doctor's "treatment." Her friend said he did the same thing to her, and she thought it was weird. "I felt more courage then," Larissa tells me. "And I felt protective of her. That's when I said, 'I'm going to say something.'"

Larissa went to the head coach of the Michigan State gymnastics team, Kathie Klages. Sitting in her office, "I told her in detail," Larissa says. "I said, 'His fingers are going inside of me and it feels like he is fingering me.'" The meeting did not go well. "The worst part was Kathie's reaction," she says. Larissa felt interrogated, then publicly humiliated, as the coach started calling other gymnasts from the youth program into the room, in pairs or in groups of three, asking if they felt uncomfortable with treatments from Larry. Larissa had to sit there, embarrassed.

Larissa told the coach that Larry had done the same thing to another gymnast, and so the coach talked to the other gymnast as well. The young girl said yes, the doctor had put his fingers inside her too. Larissa recalls that the coach said the girls must have misunderstood the treatment, because Larry wouldn't do anything inappropriate. Then the coach enlisted some of the gymnasts from the college team, Larissa says, asking them to talk with Larissa privately while the coach left the room. She remembers hearing them say, "His hands get close to certain areas, but they never go inside." She replied, "Well, that's not what's happening to me. It feels like he's fingering me." When the coach returned, Larissa remained adamant. "I told her, 'I'm telling the truth,'" she says. "I felt like I had to prove I'm not a liar."

The coach told Larissa she could file a report but warned that there would be "serious consequences" for both Larissa and the doctor, she says. At this point, Larissa adds, "I just wanted to get out of her office." The coach, who had known Larry for years, previously working with him at Great Lakes Gymnastics, did not notify the two girls' parents and did not talk to authorities, Larissa says. Instead, the coach told Larry what the girls had said.

"That just gave him so much confidence and power," Larissa says.

She remembers the terrible sinking feeling when she realized, at her next appointment with Larry, that the coach had betrayed her confidence, feeding her back to "the wolf." Larry sat down across from her and said, ominously, "Well. I talked to Kathie." Then he lectured her, saying that he was performing a treatment that would help her. Feeling mortified, ashamed, and in trouble for what she had done, she apologized to him for the misunderstanding. She said it was all her fault. Then she hopped back up on the massage table to prove that she didn't have a dirty mind for thinking he had done something sexual. His abuse that day was "really rough," she tells me. "I felt like he was mad at me." She lay on the table, feeling defeated. She had been silenced.

Larry continued to abuse her for four years. Sometimes he asked about her sex life and how often she gave her boyfriend a "blowjob." She told him she wasn't sexually active, but he insisted that she must do it all the time. She wasn't even sure what he was talking about. Looking back, she remembers that once, he turned the lights off, removed his belt, and made grunting sounds; she believes he was masturbating. She tried to get off the table, but he pushed her back down by the head and told her not to move. She slid into depression. "At first, I felt like I ruined all my chances for competing in college. I wanted to go to MSU," she says. But as the abuse continued over time, she says, "I lost my love for the sport."

She went on to have suicidal thoughts. In court, she shared a journal entry from when she was seventeen:

> Slowly day by day it is creeping up on me, always one step closer to devouring my soul. I feel so unworthy of living and being happy. I am always feeling the guilt of something which gets heavier as each day passes. It's almost as if I have a pile of bricks weighing down on my shoulders. Every day a new one is added on my weary back. I am tired of being so unhappy with things in my life right now. I even feel guilty for feeling guilty. I guess that I am just a mental case. Will these feelings change and leave me in peace, or will I have to live with this the rest of my life?

Years later, when the *Indianapolis Star* ran the allegations against Larry in 2016, Larissa didn't want to believe them—even though she had once reported the abuse herself. She wanted to believe that the doctor had performed a legitimate medical treatment. It was too painful to think that she had been right about the abuse as a child, she tells me, and that he had gone on hurting girls for all those years. She recalls how she walked the Michigan State campus, visiting the field house where she had practiced, taking in the sounds and smells from when she was a young gymnast, and coming to terms with the truth. "It gave me chills," she says. "I finally began to accept that I was right all those years ago. I was able to allow myself to revisit the past in detail, including many of the different times the abuse happened."

Larissa turned to local attorney Manvir "Mick" Grewal for help. She had known him for years—he was her next-door neighbor when she was a child. When I meet with Mick at his office in a quiet, grassy suburb of Lansing to talk about the case, he greets me with a warm smile, then sits down and tells me how he remembers seeing young Larissa bouncing on the trampoline with friends in her backyard. The poignant childhood image makes him sad now, because Larissa was in the grips of a predator at the time, but he had no idea.

When Larissa went to see Mick amid the Nassar scandal, she wanted him to know that she had reported Larry back in 1997, to no avail. The gymnast who had reported Larry with her (who wishes to remain anonymous) met with Mick as well. When they shared their stories, Mick recalls, "You could see the anguish, thinking they might not be believed." But he believed. Empathy is in his blood, he says. The son of a doctor and nurse who moved to America from the Punjab region of India, he tells me that his name, Manvir, means "one who people will confide their secrets to." When he heard the women's stories, he says, "It pained me to see how much they were hurting, and that few believed them." It would become a key theme in the Nassar case: women dismissed and disbelieved throughout the decades. It disturbed him deeply. Growing up in the Sikh religion, he had learned from an early age that women and men are equal, a key tenet of the faith. Many more women would walk through his door, and he would eventually represent more than a hundred, he says, noting that he considers them to be family. "Part of my culture, heritage, religion is that my middle name is Singh. Singh means lion. That is my trademark," he says. "A lion protects its family."

Before I leave his office, he hands me a teal T-shirt—the color of sexual assault awareness. The names of all the sister survivors, as the women call themselves, are emblazoned in white on the back. Mick had the T-shirts made to show his support, and he gave them out to his clients, their families, and others "all across the country, even a few overseas," he tells me. "It helped survivors know they have support all over the world."

When Larissa gave her victim impact statement in court, with her father and husband by her side, she spoke with confidence and conviction, her voice steady as she faced her abuser. She described her mind-set in the years after the abuse. "My thinking was so warped and confused, as I had rewired my thought process to believe I was wrong for thinking of things sexually," she said. Years later, she recalled, "I graduated from Michigan State University. I then applied for physical therapy school, and Larry was one of the ones that wrote me a letter of recommendation for the doctoral program." Turning to Larry, she said, "I don't know if you remember that."

"I remember," he replied.

She explained how the realization that her childhood instincts had been right—and that Larry could have been stopped in 1997—had caused tremendous physical and emotional fallout, including panic attacks, shingles, depression, migraines, and other serious problems. "My heart hurts. My body hurts. My mind hurts. My family hurts," she said. "My entire life has been affected."

Her husband and father spoke in court too, describing the effects of the abuse on the family. "There is nothing in life that can prepare someone to help their spouse through emotional trauma this intense," her husband, Adam Boyce, said, recalling a terrifying moment in the early months of the scandal when Larissa said she had thoughts of suicide. "My worldview has been significantly and forever altered," he said. "I have a difficult time trusting my children to anyone. I often have terrible thoughts of rage towards this awful human being whom I've never met. I have trouble going to sleep at night and wake up in the middle of the night with my mind racing. My blood pressure is higher. I have less patience. I am working through a temporary state of depression—temporary— that was thrust upon me."

Together, the family is helping each other heal and move forward. "Through time, my pain and sadness will get easier," Larissa said in court, addressing Larry with an unflinching gaze. "Today, I can finally say that I am free from the hold you had over me. Today, I am seizing the power and control you took from me."

Afterward, Judge Aquilina praised Larissa for her courage, saying, "The world has heard every word, and your words are very clear and very brave. And your thinking has never been confused. So at some point, I don't know if you've done this already or not, and no, I'm not a therapist, but I do know that you need to forgive that sixteen-year-old, that girl who didn't know because you trusted the wrong people. And that happens all the time to children, so your message is being delivered. We need to teach our children to question and re-question, and we need adults to speak loudly on behalf of children. You have killed the beast that you were afraid of with your strength and your words."

Today, Larissa tells me, she dreams of creating a healing retreat center for people who have survived sexual abuse. "I want it to be peaceful and holistic, with animals, horses, art therapy," she says. "It's a very big dream, but the dream has been born."

Her former coach Kathie Klages, meanwhile, got suspended and then resigned from Michigan State after the Nassar scandal hit the news. After Nassar was sentenced, she was charged with lying to the police, accused of falsely denying that she had been informed of the abuse. She has pleaded not guilty.

I sought comment from Kathie Klages, via her attorneys, on the allegations cited in this book. An attorney replied, "Mrs. Klages is innocent of the allegations lodged against her, and we believe that this will be proven at her trial."

Tragically, Larissa was not the last girl to be silenced.

Chapter Seven

The Scream

As the nineties drew to a close, young women and girls continued to speak out against the doctor, hoping someone would listen. Sixteen-year-old Lindsey Schuett actually *screamed* out against him in 1999. Her experience unfolded like a scene from a horror movie.

Lindsey was a gymnast and a new kid in town—her family had just moved from South Dakota—when she went to the Michigan State clinic for chronic hip pain. A doctor began seeing her there but soon transferred her to Larry—at Larry's request. He had noticed Lindsey at the clinic and said he could use his expertise in treating gymnasts to help.

Now in her thirties and living in South Korea, where she teaches English to kids in an immersive village, Lindsey tells me her story from her bedroom across the world, via FaceTime. She recalls being impressed to learn that Larry worked with Olympians, including her hero, Kerri Strug. "She's the whole reason I got into gymnastics," she says.

Lindsey's first appointment with Larry was odd, she says, recalling how he told her mother, "Some people complain that I'm too hands-on, but I really care about my patients." Then, she says, "He reached back and slapped me on my behind a couple times."

She felt uneasy, but he was the big-deal Olympic doctor, and she didn't dwell on it.

At her next appointment, Larry handed her a pair of loose shorts to wear, then told her to lie on the massage table. Her mom sat and waited in the same room, reading a book, while the doctor massaged Lindsey's sides and legs. "He moved up my leg and got up to the shorts area. I remember thinking, He's touching my panty line; this is getting uncomfortable. Then he went under my shorts, and I started to lose it. You're trying to tell yourself, It's OK, it's gonna stop, he's not gonna cross the line. Then he crossed the line. It became real. He was freely penetrating me, and it was terrible, long and excruciating." She knew about sexual abuse. She had seen the movie *The Hand That Rocks the Cradle*, in which a doctor sexually molests a young woman. It had just happened to her, and she knew it.

After the distressing experience, she tried to figure out how to proceed. "I was new at school. I thought, Everybody will hate me if I accuse him," she says. The kids were already teasing her for being from South Dakota, calling her a hick. After a few nights of crying herself to sleep, she found the courage to tell her school counselor, fearing that if she didn't speak up, she would get sent back to the doctor. The counselor listened and told her to call her parents, handing her the phone. Lindsey did so, and her mom said they would discuss it later. Lindsey still worried that she would have to see Larry again. She shared this fear with her counselor once again. "She said she doubted that would happen, but if it did, then I should tell him very nicely that I didn't like the treatment," Lindsey says. The counselor didn't take the report of abuse any further. "She thought she had done her job because she had me tell my parents. She never followed up with me."

Lindsey did not end up having that discussion with her mom about Larry, she says, because her parents were busy and distracted. But she did ask her mother if she would have to see him again, making her anxiety clear. Her mother didn't say. A young, vulnerable teen, Lindsey worried that she was no match for the doctor, who had the backing of powerful institutions in both Michigan State and USA Gymnastics and was roundly trusted and respected. Her voice was not heard, just as she had feared.

One dreadful day, she found herself back in the car with her mother, heading for Larry's massage table. "When I was walking in the parking lot to the office, I was thinking, What am I gonna do? I can't let him do this to me again. I thought, If he does it, I'm gonna scream," she says. Back on his table, he began his slow massage, and the nightmare started. "The whole time he's building up with this massage, I'm thinking, If he does it, I will scream," she says. "Then he finally did it. The moment he started to penetrate me, I screamed—but I couldn't get that loud of a scream out. He said, 'Are you OK?' I said, 'No. It hurts. Don't do that.' He said, 'Well, we're going to try it again.' And he started to penetrate me again. I screamed and cried; I didn't stop. I wanted everybody to hear me." Larry quickly hustled her out of the room and referred her to another doctor. She kept screaming as she walked down the hall and out of the clinic, just to be sure she was heard.

In the next few months, she says, "I made some friends and talked to a few people about it. The consensus was, there's no way you'll win against a guy like that. I told myself that maybe it was just me. Maybe he's scared now because I made so much noise. Maybe people looked into what he was doing." The experience caused a rift in her relationship with her parents, and when she later graduated from Michigan State, she took the opportunity to head to the other side of the world and teach English to kids, an experience she has come to love. "I ended up finding my passion," she says, but the abuse from her childhood lingered, and the family remained fractured.

Lindsey gave her victim impact statement in court by video from South Korea, recalling the moment she decided to rescue herself from the doctor: "I was going to scream and wail until he never touched me again," she said. "I was going to sob so loudly that not only did it match the screaming anger I felt inside, but it would alert every single person in that building that something was incredibly wrong in that doctor's office." She described the effects of the ordeal over time, saying, "I shall share just a few of the many ways that my life has been marred. I distrust men. I disrespect my body in many ways because I don't feel it has value. I become irrationally emotional when trying to express a problem with an authority figure. These experiences have had a serious negative effect on my family, my health, my personal life, and my professional life." Then she addressed the judge, saying, "And so now we come to the question of: How much is a young girl's quality of life worth? If anyone deserves to never see the light of day again, it is this man." Lindsey's poignant question on the worth of a girl became a defining phrase for the survivors throughout the court hearings and beyond.

After watching the searing video statement, Judge Aquilina blasted off a red-hot response. "I want her to know that her screaming is being heard all the way in 2018," she said. "Her question really resonates with me. I will decide at sentencing how long. The plea agreement, which as I said, I will honor, but on the tail end, I'll make that determination: How much is a young girl's life worth? Our Constitution does not allow for cruel and unusual punishment. If it did, I have to say, I might allow what he did to all of these beautiful souls—these young women in their childhood—I would allow someone or many people to do to him what he did to others." She continued, "Our country does not have an eye for an eye, and Michigan doesn't have the death penalty, so I don't know how to answer how much is a young girl's life worth, but I have children of my own, and there's not enough gold in the planet that would satisfy that question. And I think all of you victims are gold. You're valuable. I'm so very sorry this happened, and, Lindsey, I've heard your scream."

Three student athletes at Michigan State also reported the abuse starting in the late nineties: softball player Tiffany Thomas Lopez, cross-country runner Christie Achenbach, and volleyball player Jennifer Bedford. All three say they told employees at the university that they were uncomfortable with the invasive proced-ure, according to an investigation of the school launched by the Michigan attorney general after the Nassar sentencing in 2018.

In fact, the three athletes are among thirteen women who say they reported the abuse to Michigan State employees over the course of nearly two decades, according to the investigation. The women say they told eleven employees at the university—athletic trainers, coaches, counselors, and doctors—to no avail. The investi-gators interviewed the employees in question, finding the following:

> Nearly every employee either claimed that they could not recall receiving a report of abuse, or explicitly denied ever being told. Although there is no evidence that these MSU employees consciously conspired with each other or with Nassar to cover up his abuse, the real explanation of why Nassar was able to perpetrate his crimes for so long is little better. In some sense, the MSU employees around Nassar were misled much like the survivors were. All of Nassar's colleagues stated that they never witnessed Nassar digitally penetrate a patient, though the ones most familiar with Nas-sar's specialty emphasized that vaginal penetration could be medically appropriate in certain, rare circumstances. . . . It is evident that Nassar was able to use his associates' familiarity with a legitimate medical technique to conduct treatment that resembled that technique, but which constituted sexual assault, done for his own personal sexual gratification.

Nonetheless, the investigation found, employees who reportedly were told of the invasive procedure "downplayed its seriousness or affirmatively discouraged the survivors from proceeding with their allegation." The investigators noted the following:

> That so many survivors independently disclosed to so many different MSU employees over so many years, each time with no success, reveals a problem that cannot be explained as mere isolated, individual failures; it is evidence of a larger cultural problem at the MSU Sports Medicine Clinic and MSU more broadly. For as varied as the details of the survivors' accounts are, there is a common thread through each: the tendency of MSU employees to give the benefit of the doubt to Nassar, not the young women who came forward. When faced with accusations of digital penetration during routine medical treatments—serious allegations that amount to criminal wrongdoing—the MSU employees discounted the young woman's story and deferred to Nassar, the world-renowned sports medicine doctor.

The bottom line: Larry, the all-important doctor, was widely trusted. The young women were not.

I contacted the Michigan State media relations department, citing the allegations in this book and seeking comment, but did not receive a response. I did hear back from a former member of the media team who now works in a different department at the university; he said he would send my request to the media staff, but still, no response.

"I remember laying there wondering, Is this OK? This doesn't seem right," Jennifer Bedford, the former volleyball player, said in her victim impact statement in court, describing how Larry abused her at an appointment while casually chatting away. "There were two arguments at war in my mind: this doesn't seem right, versus, he's a world-renowned doctor who's treated so many athletes," she said. "Everyone knows he treats 'down there,' and they don't complain, so just stop being a baby." Her teammates knew of his unorthodox methods, jokingly calling him the "crotch doc."

Jennifer, standing in court with her husband by her side, his hand resting on her back, described herself as a sheltered athlete at the time. Then she described another layer to the abuse she endured: her body physically responded against her will. "Originally I was very hesitant to share the details of this part," she said. "But I think this is a huge problem in society today, that there are people that are hesitant to speak up, because they think a victim wanted to be assaulted, and that's just not true." She continued, "To be clear, during that appointment, Larry put direct pressure on places I didn't know existed at the time, and my body reacted. I didn't want it to, but it reacted anyways. And as it was happening, I remember laying there, frozen stiff on the table, utterly mortified, confused, and scared. I felt so powerless to control what was happening."

Larry pretended not to notice. "In the aftermath, questions raced through my mind a mile a minute, trying to make sense of it all. Could my body really react that way if I didn't want it to? I thought that was impossible," she said in court. "I felt like my body had just betrayed me. I had built up such a wall of protection in my mind around Larry that my first reaction was to question myself, to blame myself. I wanted to believe the best in people, but no matter how much I rationalized—he's a doctor, he's trying to help you, you should be grateful he's treating you, he didn't mean for it to happen—I couldn't shake the voice in my head that said something wasn't right."

When Jennifer thought about reporting the doctor, fear set in—fear of being called a liar, being looked down on, being labeled, being called "messed up." She did talk to her trainer, she said in court, asking if she could file a complaint, and the trainer asked her some questions. "I tried to answer as truthfully as possible, but I was so scared of revealing what I thought were shameful details that I didn't give her much to go on. In the end, she wanted me to understand that filing a report would involve an investigation, making an accusation against Nassar, and stating that I felt he did something unprofessional or criminally wrong. At the time, I couldn't say. . . I had a hard time saying that with certainty. I just wanted to say I was uncomfortable and have it recorded. I wasn't aware of a way to do that without making a formal accusation and exposing those mortifying details to the world."

Jennifer, in her scalding twenty-five-minute statement, said that looking back now, she wonders if she could have stopped the doctor from continuing his abuse. She concluded, "I want to stand with all the women who came forward before me and after me, if just to say, you're not alone. I'm speaking up for my loved ones, for my nieces, my nephews, my family, brothers, sisters, friends. I pray they would never find themselves in similar circumstances, but should that day come, I want them to be courageous, truthful, to speak up without shame. I'm speaking simply to stand for truth and to face fear, and to refuse to give fear a foothold any longer."

Tiffany Thomas Lopez, the former softball player, spoke poignantly in her court statement of the emotional pain she endured as well. Confronting her betrayer, she said, "I imagined hitting you if I ever had the opportunity to see you again. Instead, I'll allow my thoughts and my feelings to hit your heart. You, and your actions, have walked with me every step of the way since leaving Michigan State University, such a beautiful campus tarnished with your touch." She described sobbing on the massage table, feeling violated, while Larry asked her what was wrong. She said she had wondered over the years if she had been the only one or if there had been others. "Every few years I wondered if there was another Tiffany Thomas," she said in court. "But to my surprise, I'd find pictures of you smiling and enjoying life. I was hurt and disappointed but also extremely relieved knowing it was only me, and I accepted this as something I would live with forever."

She told Larry, "I have decided to start living again. Your actions have had me by the throat for years, and I am ready to be released by your clench. I will no longer fear speaking up for myself. I will no longer fear speaking up for my children. I will stand my ground to those in authoritative positions. And most importantly, I will try not to be hesitant toward male medical professionals. I will try to forgive you of your wrongdoing and allow my heart to heal."

In closing, she looked at Larry and said, with a cool resolve, that she and the army of survivors would prevail. "The army you chose in the late nineties to silence me, to dismiss me and my attempt at speaking the truth, will not prevail over the army you created when violating us. We seek justice. We deserve justice, and we will have it."

She was right. But back then, justice was a long way off. Larry would sharpen his skills in the next decade, becoming a master predator.

Chapter Eight

The Seduction

As Larry marched into a new decade in 2000, he became an expert at grooming and seducing the parents of his young patients. He also became a father himself, welcoming his first of three children to the world in 2001, a baby girl. All the while, young women and girls kept reporting his abuse to people in positions of authority—including the police.

Lindsey Lemke's story illustrates how he masterfully manipulated the parents as well as the kids. She started gymnastics in 2002, when she was six years old, a sandy-haired, hazel-eyed kid growing up in Bay City, Michigan, a scenic city of bridges and boats, where the Saginaw River runs into a bay of Lake Huron. The sport had caught her eye while she was taking a dance class. When she saw a gymnast flying through the air in another class, she knew what she wanted to do. Her mom signed her up for gymnastics at a local gym called Bay Valley Academy, and Lindsey got her first leotard, stretchy and silky. She loved it so much, she wore it to bed.

"I never wanted to take it off," she says. "I wanted to do everything in it." With her enthusiasm and natural talent, she became the star of the gym. When she was around eight years old, she recalls, her coach told her, "You should go down to Twistars and have a coach look at you there." Twistars, the gymnastics club

John Geddert had launched in Dimondale, was about an hour and a half away from Lindsey's hometown. Her mom drove her there for the tryouts.

"Holy crap," Lindsey said when she walked into the gym. "This place is huge." Twistars was an impressive gymnastics factory by now, producing scores of top athletes. Lindsey heard grunts and thuds and coaches yelling. The kids looked super-focused as they propelled themselves around bars and vaults, landing on thick, bright mats. The place smelled like sweat. She immediately sensed the competitive vibe. Her little hometown gym had been fun, and she had easily excelled; no one yelled at anyone there. This gym was clearly a different ballgame. Still, she didn't let herself feel intimidated. She wanted to show what she could do, and she figured she had nothing to lose. She kept her composure and aced the tryouts.

Lindsey and I first met in the spring of 2017, just a few months after the Nassar scandal burst into the news—before the guilty pleas and all the victim impact statements in court. Dozens of women had come forward at this point, talking to police and attorneys, but many wished to remain anonymous. Lindsey was one of the first to publicly identify herself. It took courage. Trolls were on Twitter, attacking away. Lindsey saw snarky posts on Facebook, questioning the gymnasts and their parents, calling them clueless. She was a junior at Michigan State at the time, twenty-one years old, a gymnast on the team with a full scholarship. She and her mother, Christy Lemke-Akeo, wanted people to understand how predators operate.

When we first met, Lindsey and her mom still seemed a bit shell-shocked by the double life of Larry Nassar. Over the next year, that would change. They would move into a different phase—anger and frustration, not just at Larry, but at all the people who enabled him. They would become an increasingly powerful and outspoken force for accountability and change. But that first time we talked, when they were still trying to wrap their heads around all of it, they gave me raw insight into Larry's evolution.

It's an early Saturday morning when I meet Lindsey and Christy at the office of their family friend and attorney, Jamie White, just outside of Lansing. Gymnasts like to start the day early. Lindsey looks calm, focused. Jamie brings Lindsey her favorite bacon-onion-cheese biscuit from McDonald's, and she tells me very matter-of-factly the story of how she and her parents got ensnared by Larry.

In her first few months at Twistars, she says, she felt years behind the other gymnasts, some of whom had started practicing when they were just toddlers. She wanted to catch up. Her mom began driving her to the gym every day after school. Her schedule became insane. It went like this: Bolt out of school after the final class of the day. Do homework in the car. Arrive at the gym around five o'clock in the afternoon. Practice till nine at night. Drive home with her mom, getting back to Bay City before midnight. Fall into bed and get up and do it all over again. Parents weren't allowed to hang out in the gym, but there was a room overlooking the gym, where they could sit and read a book, work out, or observe the training through a window, although they couldn't hear from up there.

Lindsey's mom, Christy, petite and vivacious, says the family was willing to make the sacrifice so Lindsey could follow her dreams. But it wasn't easy. Christy worked as a dental office manager, and her husband was a project manager at General Motors. They had a young son as well. All the driving back and forth was a logistical challenge. "I moved my schedule around and drove her down there every day," Christy recalls. They just made it work. Sometimes, she and Lindsey would stay overnight at the Comfort Inn down the road from the gym.

The coaches at Twistars hounded Lindsey, making her repeat techniques till she nailed them. When she didn't, she got sentenced to extra rope climbs. Rope climbs were hell. There were various levels of difficulty, such as climbing the rope using only hands, no legs—the girls would climb with their legs out to one side or the other, or in splits. When they mastered that, they would do the same climb but with a weighted vest. And sometimes they would be timed too. "I thought, Yeah, it sucked to have to do that stuff, but I assumed that if I wanted to be good, that this is what I had to do. So I just went along with it, no matter how hard it got. I was a pretty obedient kid." She pauses and adds, "When you're so dedicated and disciplined at that age, and you want to perform well, you're willing to do anything. So it's like, if this is what it takes to become a Level 10 gymnast, then this is what it takes," she says, referring to the highest skill level in the Junior Olympic realm.

Her mom was surprised by Lindsey's determination. "I would've been out of there. I would've been like, peace out," she says. "She just took it upon herself and kept going. I mean, we would tell her, 'If you want to quit, then quit.' We were pretty laid-back. We always said this to our kids, and I say it to them now: if you're not having fun, stop doing what you're doing and move on to something else." Lindsey kept scrambling up and down the ropes. She got rope burns on her skin while the shouts from John rang in her ears, telling her she wasn't trying hard enough. "I thought, He won't give me a break unless there's a bone sticking out of my body," she says. She had in fact noticed that girls kept training with injuries. The girls were there to win. John drilled this into their heads: When you go to a meet, you win. Period. Lindsey kept hustling.

*****

Around the time Lindsey was getting indoctrinated at Twistars, Larry's wife gave birth to the couple's second child, another girl.

Also at this time, in 2004, seventeen-year-old Brianne Randall reported Larry to the police.

Brianne had gone to see him for help with a scoliosis condition that was causing chronic back pain, she tells me. She was an athlete who played soccer and tennis, not a gymnast, and she had met with him at the Michigan State clinic, where he saw patients from across the Lansing community. "I felt really lucky to see him because of his status as the Olympic coach," she tells me. "He came highly recommended to us."

He gave her a gown and a pair of shorts to wear, then "proceeded to penetrate me vaginally and massage my breasts," she said in her victim impact statement, recounting the ordeal. "My body froze. I was screaming inside but lay there too scared and confused to do anything." Afterward, alone in the room with her, the doctor scheduled more appointments with her. Then he asked her for a hug. "When I got home from school that day, I told my mom what had happened. She took me to the police station, where I filed a report and went to the hospital to get a sexual assault kit done," she said in her statement. "I was terrified of what this exam entailed. I sat in a cold hospital room; my body tensed when they took the samples. I remember fearing that no one would believe me. Unfortunately, this fear became a reality."

Larry told detectives Andrew McCready and Bart Crane at the Meridian Township Police Department that the invasive procedure was a legitimate medical treatment, according to the police report. He didn't deny touching Brianne; he said he did it on purpose. He threw around some medical jargon in the interview with the detectives, then sent them a PowerPoint presentation he had written about his technique, laced with more medical lingo. The PowerPoint file, which is attached to the police report, makes your head spin—a blizzard of x-rays, illustrations, and impenetrable medical-speak. The police report doesn't say whether the detectives questioned the doctor about the breast massage. The detectives did not interview any medical experts about the doctor's methods.

Instead, the detectives believed the doctor—bam—and closed the case. They did not forward it to the prosecutor's office. Detective McCready called Brianne's mother and announced that they were done. There would be "no prosecution being sought, due to the facts presented to me by Dr. Nassar," he told her, according to the police report. Brianne's mom replied that she was concerned about the doctor's behavior, particularly the fact that he hadn't used gloves for the procedure. Detective McCready said he would pass along her concerns to the doctor.

And just like that, Brianne was dismissed.

Brianne revisited the nightmarish experience in her victim impact statement, taking a slow, deep breath before addressing Larry directly in court. "Mr. Nassar, do I look familiar to you? Do you recognize my name? I was a seventeen-year-old that reported your abuse to police in 2004. You used my vulnerability at the time to sexually abuse me," she said. "The police questioned you, and you had the audacity to tell them I had misunderstood this treatment because I was not comfortable with my body. How *dare* you. Sadly, they took your word instead of mine. I am here today to tell you I wasn't afraid of you then, and I'm sure as hell not afraid of you now. Your power has been taken from you by an army of strong women."

Now a physician's assistant, Brianne implored that parents, police, and institutions "please listen to children when they report abuse, and take action." She added, "Mr. Nassar's abuse went on for too long because nobody was listening to us. The time is up for you, Mr. Nassar, and for all perpetrators."

Judge Aquilina thanked her for her important message, adding, "You are a hero. You are a survivor, and you are a part of this strong army that's only getting stronger."

Soon after Brianne spoke in court, Meridian Township officials publicly apologized to her in a press conference. "I want to start, first of all, with the most important reason we're here, and that's to apologize, on behalf of the community, our police department, to you, Brianne. We failed you. We let you down," said Meridian Township manager Frank Walsh, noting that he had been with the township since 2013. "I know we've had a lot of private conversations, private apologies, but we felt this needed to be done in public." He also publicly apologized to her mother, husband, and other family members, saying, "You've all been through a lot, and we are sorry for that."

Meridian Township officials later commissioned an independent investigation of the case, releasing the findings in 2019. The investigation sought to answer key questions from Brianne, such as why the detectives had failed to interview any medical experts before closing the case. As of this writing, the two detectives who had interviewed Larry Nassar in the case, Andrew McCready and Bart Crane, are both employed as sergeants with the Meridian Township Police. Sergeant McCready told the independent investigators that he had not consulted any medical experts in the case because he had believed the doctor's lies.

I contacted the Meridian Township Police to see if Sergeant McCready and Sergeant Crane would like to comment on their handling of the case for this book. A police lieutenant replied that he had sent my query to both sergeants and that they had declined to comment.

Brianne received a phone call and a personal apology from Sergeant McCready, leaving her with "complicated" feelings, she tells me. "To be honest, it was an awkward conversation. I don't know him, so I don't know how he feels about this or his sincerity. He seemed sincere on the phone, and I accepted his apology. That's not to say that I'm not still angry. I don't think there's a day that goes by, or a day that will go by, that I won't think about this. It's always with me, no matter how much I want to forget it."

Still, she has empathy for him. "Some days I'm angry, and other days I feel sorry for the detective. I live with extreme guilt every day that I wasn't able to stop Larry and that because of that, hundreds of other girls were abused. Because I, unlike many others, knew that it was abuse. For over a decade I knew I was abused, and I felt powerless in stopping it. So the guilt, it's with me every day. Like

I said, as guilty as I feel, I can't imagine the overwhelming guilt the detective must feel. I think this has been hard for him, understandably. Although I'm mad at him, I hate that this has ruined or at least changed his life too. I don't want to see that happen to anyone, no matter how angry I may be with them."

Indeed, if the police had listened to young Brianne back in 2004, Larry would have never met hundreds of other girls.

But Brianne wasn't the only girl to report Larry that year.

Twelve-year-old Kyle Stephens did so as well. In her scorching victim impact statement in court, she said she was six years old, a fan of Clifford the Big Red Dog, when Larry, a close friend of her family, began targeting her. "He first exposed his penis to me in a dark boiler room of the basement of his home," she said. "He told me, 'If you ever want to see it, all you have to do is ask.' He used his power as an adult to manipulate me. Over a six-year period, he progressed from exposure to masturbating in front of me while playing hide-and-go-seek, rubbing his bare penis on my bare feet, and penetrating my vagina with his fingers. All of which took place with my parents, my sibling, his wife, and his children in the same house." She said the smell of the brand of lotion he used to masturbate still makes her sick.

Kyle realized something was wrong at age twelve, when she learned about the priest-abuse scandal in the news and, separately, a friend confided her own abuse. Kyle told her parents that when Larry rubbed her feet, he used his penis. "My parents confronted him, and he denied any such action," she said in court. He convinced them that he was innocent. Turning to Larry in court, Kyle reminded him of the mind games he played with her when she was a child: "After my parents confronted you, they brought you back to my house to speak with me. Sitting on my living room couch, I listened to you tell me, 'No one should ever do that, and if they do, you should tell someone.' Well, Larry, I'm here, not to tell someone, but to tell *everyone*."

At the time, her parents sent her to speak with a psychologist at Michigan State, Dr. Gary Stollak, who failed to inform authorities about her report of abuse. Years later, after the Nassar scandal erupted, he agreed to permanently surrender his license to treat patients. He has said he has no memory of meeting with Kyle due to a stroke, according to the *Detroit News*.[8]

Kyle's relationship with her parents unraveled. "I spent the years between twelve and eighteen avoiding and detaching from my family," she said in court, noting that her relationship with her father was especially tense. "His belief that I had lied seeped into the foundation of our relationship. Every time we got into a fight, he would tell me, 'You need to apologize to Larry.'" When she was around fourteen, she was prodded into babysitting for the Nassar kids and began to feel "brainwashed" at his home. "It was as if I had never accused him. I thought I was losing my grip on reality. I started to question whether the abuse ever really happened. For my own sanity, I forced myself to walk through the abuse, step by step, so I didn't forget that I was not a liar."

Just before leaving for college, in yet another clash with her father, she told him she had not lied as a child, and finally, he understood and believed. "Larry Nassar's actions had already caused me significant anguish, but I hurt worse as I watched my father realize what he had put me through," she said in court. She and her father began repairing their relationship, but tragically, in 2016, he committed suicide. "Admittedly, my father was experiencing debilitating health issues, but had he not had to bear the shame and self-loathing that stemmed from his defense of Larry Nassar, I believe he would have had a fighting chance for his life. Larry Nassar wedged himself between myself and my family and used his leverage as my parents' trusted friend to pry us apart until we fractured."

She told Larry in court, staring him down with her eyes ablaze, "I have been coming for you for a long time."

*****

While Kyle and Brianne were getting dismissed and disbelieved in 2004, Lindsey Lemke was starting her own march toward Larry Nassar.

Lindsey pushed herself hard at Twistars, trying to catch up to the other girls. Her mom became concerned about the intensity of it all. "I told her, 'You don't have to do this,'" Christy says. "You can stop anytime." But Lindsey wanted to keep going. She dreamed of getting stronger and sharper, aiming for Level 10. Still, she had such a long way to go, it got overwhelming. One morning in the shower, feeling physically and mentally spent, she started crying uncontrollably. She was tired of feeling sore, tired of feeling tired. She felt she could never catch up. When her mom asked her what was wrong, she said, "I don't want to do gymnastics anymore."

"Then quit," Christy said. Lindsey said no. She didn't really want to give up. Instead, she started taking private lessons in addition to her workouts at Twistars. Her parents paid some $800 a month for coaching and other fees, and she appreciated their support. The family was deeply invested now. She began competing in meets, gaining skills and confidence with each competition.

Like Sara Teristi before her, Lindsey had the drive. But also like Sara, she said something else was at play—training that felt more like brainwashing. "You weren't allowed to have an opinion, a voice," she says. "If I had a bad day at practice, my confidence would be shot in the ground." While Lindsey pushed herself to have more good days, Sara, in her early thirties at this point and living in Colorado, was trying to never think about gymnastics ever again. She had just met her future husband, and she continued to bury her past.

After a couple of years of driving to Twistars, Lindsey's family decided to move to Lansing to be closer to the gym. Her parents knew she was committed to the sport, and the three-hour round-trip drive was wearing everyone out. They decided it was worth it to uproot. At this point, Lindsey began going to Twistars twice a day—both before and after school, for hours at a time. In all, she spent more than thirty hours a week in the gym. She became a machine. She told herself, Keep going. This is what it takes.

Her dad transferred to a new job at General Motors in Lansing, while her mom found a position at a dental office, then later started her own housecleaning business. Among her clients: attorney Jamie White and his wife, Christine. They all became friends, and Christy shared stories and pictures of Lindsey's triumphs in gymnastics. Little did Christy know that one day, she and her daughter would be enlisting Jamie's help.

Meanwhile, Larry's wife gave birth to the couple's third and final child, a boy, in 2006. Larry started a charity, the Gymnastics Doctor Autism Foundation; his first daughter has autism, which he had written about on Facebook.

Lindsey became consumed with training and school. Her friends were her fellow gymnasts at Twistars; they understood her universe, where girls lived and breathed gymnastics while their coaches bossed them around. Sure, the girls felt competitive with each other, Lindsey says, but they supported each other too. They were all in this weird world together. They were family.

When she turned ten, Lindsey hit a hot streak, winning state and regional championships. Over the next few years, she racked up more wins and reached Level 10, achieving her goal. She loved traveling around the country with her teammates to the meets. These were good times. Her hard work had paid off. But the expectations of her grew too. Once, when she bungled a vault, she says, John picked up a mat and hit her with it. She also saw him shove other girls and throw things at them, she says, including water bottles and, once, a bag of ice, hurled at a girl's head. Sometimes, she says, he would take a girl by the shoulders, squeezing hard while shouting in her face. Another time, when he was mad at the Level 10 gymnasts, he made them clean the locker room and filmed them with a video camera to embarrass them. "He was in a mood that day," Lindsey says. Yet this was the only world she knew; she had learned that the important thing was to win, to keep the coach happy. The coach looked good if the girls won. She kept striving for wins.

Things started to go south when she landed badly after a back-flip with two and a half twists, rolling her ankle. Feeling a stabbing pain, she told John, "I need to stop." He disagreed, she says. "Keep going!" he yelled. She followed his orders. She moved to the uneven bars, thinking that this would take the weight off her foot, but she couldn't land her dismounts correctly. Her foot was pounding wildly. John yelled, "If your foot hurts that bad, then go get it looked at!" He sounded furious, Lindsey recalls. A regional competition was coming up, and she might miss it if she had broken a bone. She knew what he was thinking: it was her fault.

Standing outside the gym, waiting for her mom to pick her up, she began to cry—not because her foot hurt, but because John was angry at her. She felt she had let him down. She tried to shake the feeling that she was useless to him if she couldn't win. "John's mad at me," she told her mom, wiping away tears. "He kicked me out of practice." Her mother reassured her that it was not her fault. They drove to the sports medicine clinic at Michigan State to see Larry. John sent all the girls to Larry, either at the clinic or in a back room at Twistars.

The first appointment was brief, normal. She remembers that he seemed warm and friendly, sweet and dorky with dark eyes behind wire-rimmed glasses. "Yup, it's broken," he said after examining her foot. She learned she would need to wear a boot and use crutches for four to six weeks. She knew John would be mad.

She hated sitting on the sidelines but healed quickly, got back on her feet, and resumed winning. Then, when she was around twelve years old, another problem cropped up: a burning pain in her back. Suddenly, every single thing she did hurt her back. It felt painful to breathe, to bend down, to stand up. Even sleeping hurt.

When she landed on her head at a competition because the pain prevented her from doing a backflip properly, she went back to see Larry. He diagnosed her with a condition in which the vertebrae grow unevenly. He said the pain would subside when she grew, after she got through puberty. In the meantime, he said, he would massage her aching muscles to help loosen them up.

He began seeing Lindsey at weekly appointments at the clinic at Michigan State, often after hours, to accommodate her family's schedule, or so he said. "He said he would work us in because he knew we were busy," Christy says, a look of disgust on her face. "He made it sound like it was for us." He endeared himself to Lindsey, doing thoughtful little things like taking the time to drop off Advil or Icy Hot at her home. He became a mentor and confidant, offering a listening ear. If she had a bad day with her coach, she would tell him about it. If she argued with her mom, she would spill her guts about that too, either in his office or via text on her phone. When her back pain became so extreme that she thought about quitting, Larry talked her out of it. "He would just put everything into perspective. I would go to him and tell him I wanted to quit, my body hurt too much, this and that, and I'd leave that appointment and be more motivated, like I was gonna frickin' go to the Olympics and win a gold medal. He had your back through anything. He was just so nice," she says, then looks at me and adds, "You probably think I'm so messed up for saying that."

Not at all, I tell her. I can picture the battle in her brain, trying to reconcile the nice guy she knew with the monster predator now in the news. And again, she and I were talking fairly early on in the scandal, before Larry pleaded guilty and the women stood up in court. For Lindsey and her mom, it was all still sinking in.

Larry went out of his way to befriend Lindsey's parents too. He confided in them, telling them things that John Geddert had said about Lindsey and her progress. "He would fill us in on everything," Christy says. "He was kind of like the go-between the coach and the parent." In retrospect, she remembers feeling uncomfortable that he would sometimes try to discuss other gymnasts, but she didn't dwell on it because he was the Olympic doctor, the very best. He had the trust and support of Michigan State University and USA Gymnastics. Why wouldn't she trust him? Eventually, he offered to lessen the family's load by not billing their health insurer. He said he saw Lindsey's potential and wanted to help her succeed.

The family felt grateful for his thoughtfulness and care. It seemed that this highly respected doctor wanted to help Lindsey excel. "We thought, We're so lucky," Christy says, shaking her head at the memory of it. "I remember telling my family members how lucky we were that Larry was at our club. That was one of the factors that had us move down to Twistars. We knew that if Lindsey ever got injured, she would be able to see this world-renowned doctor." Lindsey felt the same. "We just felt so thankful," she recalls with a sigh. To show their appreciation for Larry, the family bought him presents, such as his favorite bottle of scotch, and gift cards to take his family out to dinner. They worried that he was spending so much time helping Lindsey, he didn't have enough time with his own kids. "We felt indebted to him," Christy says. "We were buying him gifts all the time because we felt like we were taking him away from his family time."

The appointments with Larry went the same way every time, Lindsey says. She would call or text him after hours at the clinic, and he would unlock a side door and let her in. Then he would have her lie on her stomach on a table so he could massage her back. Usually she wore shorts and a T-shirt, but once, inexplicably, he told her to take off her shorts and gave her a towel to wrap around her waist. He would use his elbow and forearm to rub up and down her back, then work his way downward toward her rear. He would knead her vagina over her shorts and then slip a hand inside the back of her shorts and start stroking her bare skin. Then he would push a finger inside her vagina, while still massaging her back with his other arm.

He claimed that if he pushed on various "pressure points," it would loosen up her inflamed muscles. The penetration lasted for fifteen to twenty minutes at a time. Larry did not wear gloves or use medical lube. He did not seek her consent or consult her parents. Lindsey had never experienced anything like this before, and it hurt. But she trusted her doctor. She believed he was performing a medical treatment. He was a celebrated physician, an authority figure, an adult in his forties. And Lindsey was a child, with little experience in the world. She thought, Who am I to question him?

She tells me this in a straightforward manner, laying out the facts without getting emotional. It's all part of her gymnastics training. Looking back to her childhood at the gym, she says, "I was never allowed to feel sorry for myself. I was never allowed to be upset when things didn't go my way. I just had to buckle down and toughen up. You know, this is life, and if this is what you want to do, this is what you have to do to get through it. I've just been trained since I was little to think like that." She seems almost stoic, and I wonder how she'll feel in a year, since the scandal is still so fresh when we first speak. Indeed, as I would later discover, a passionate, outspoken activist would emerge in the next year.

One of the ways Larry charmed the girls in his care was to give them gifts from the Olympics, such as T-shirts and pins. It reminded them that he was powerful, and it made them feel important because he saw their potential. Sometimes he brought Lindsey these Olympic souvenirs, and, like any kid, she thought that was amazing. Other times he inquired about her personal life and boys at school. She told him she had no time to think about boys. He took the time to give her greeting cards on holidays; he called or texted her on her birthday. He made her feel loved—unlike John, who made her feel she was just a robot, programmed to win. Larry seemed genuine, caring. He was like her own personal cheerleader. "He would do anything he could to make you feel like you were special," Lindsey says. "I mean, he was so much more than a doctor. He was a therapist, a friend. He didn't seem creepy. He had three kids, a family." His thoughtfulness was especially appreciated at this particular time in her life: her parents had decided to separate, and Larry was a reassuring presence.

Larry moved the appointments with Lindsey to his home. He lived just a few houses down the street from her dad, who was separated from her mom now, and he said this would be more convenient for everyone. He had the family's full trust. They considered him to be a good friend, someone who was truly looking out for Lindsey. In his basement, Larry had created a makeshift clinic. There was a massage table, like the one at the Michigan State clinic, and shelves stocked with medical equipment, medicines, tapes, braces, everything. It looked like a doctor's office. His basement was very kid-friendly as well, Lindsey recalls, with toys strewn everywhere for his three children. There were two comfy sofas, a TV, and a fireplace. Family photos lined the walls.

Lindsey began seeing him several times a week there. Occasionally she still saw him at the clinic as well or in a back room at Twistars. While the procedure never really helped with the back pain, she thought it must be medically necessary. And anyway, Larry had told her the pain would continue until she grew, so she didn't really expect it to vanish.

When her mom asked how the appointments went, Lindsey replied, "Fine." She never told her what the doctor did. The fact that Larry was a friend of her parents contributed to her thinking that everything must be OK.

Over the next four years, Larry would abuse her as many as six hundred times.

Lindsey didn't tell anyone because she didn't realize it was abuse. Like so many others, she had learned to trust doctors. And he was an Olympic doctor, no less. Why would he lie? She had never thought about sexual abuse. Her parents assumed she was sheltered and safe in her world of gymnastics; they hadn't discussed abuse.

She didn't know much about sex either; she had never even held hands with a boy. For her, dating was a long way off. "In gymnastics, we don't hang out with boys until we're frickin' juniors or seniors in high school," she says. She just kept pushing herself, winning more medals and making the Junior Olympic National Team.

Before long, Lindsey was fielding dozens of invitations for college scholarships. She visited schools around the country and felt drawn to the University of North Carolina at Chapel Hill. The idyllic campus, the warm weather—she loved it. She accepted a full-ride scholarship there. Her back pain eased up, and she figured it was because she had grown out of it, as Larry said she would.

But her freshman year did not quite go as planned. Away from home for the first time, she felt off balance, finding it difficult to keep up with the intense training and academic demands of the university. She felt far away from her family, her support system. She called her mom all the time. Her mother started traveling to visit her on the weekends.

Lindsey wanted to go home to Michigan. She wanted to live closer to her parents; she needed their support and encouragement to keep up her arduous routine. And so, she transferred to Michigan State with a full scholarship for her sophomore year. She felt she would be more comfortable there. She knew some of the gymnasts on the team, as well as some of the coaches, including the longtime head coach, Kathie Klages. She was the same coach who, according to gymnast Larissa Boyce, had learned about the abuse back in 1997 but had done nothing to stop it, a claim she has denied. But, of course, Lindsey didn't know anything about any of that. She looked forward to the years ahead at Michigan State.

Those years would be bizarre, as we will soon see.

Chapter Nine

How Kids Think

As Larry performed his "treatment" on an ever-growing number of young girls, it often worked in his favor if the girls talked to each other about it. They would decide that since he did it to everyone, it must be a legitimate medical procedure, because he wasn't singling anyone out for something inappropriate. And so the more he did it, the more he managed to protect himself.

Some girls never talked about it, such as Lindsey Lemke, but her friends Presley Allison and Taylor Stevens did. I meet with the two best friends, now in their early twenties, on a Sunday evening in Lansing, where they have just come from a barbecue. As I sit down with the two of them together, I feel a pang; it's a warm summer night, and they should be out having fun at their shindig, not talking with me about how their trusted doctor abused them as children. Taylor, green-eyed with a sprinkling of freckles, and Presley, blue-eyed with her blond hair pulled back in a loose ponytail, have been best friends since high school. They both started at Twistars in preschool, enduring the rope climbs, the yelling, the insults. Presley remembers how the girls got in trouble one time for eating frozen yogurt—deemed an unhealthy snack—at a competition and had to write letters of apology to John Geddert.

They eventually said to heck with all that and left Twistars, joining their high school gymnastics team instead. The school team, which was highly successful, winning six state championships, was a "breath of fresh air," Presley says. Taylor agrees, noting that the coach put the girls first. Both girls had seen Larry over the years for minor injuries and thought of him as a "god," Taylor says, because of his impressive credentials. It wasn't until they were in their early teens in high school that he abused them, when they both developed lower back pain.

He targeted Presley when she went to see him for treatment at his house along with her mother, who had known him for years, as her daughter had been attending Twistars from the age of five. Her mom had always accompanied her to appointments, whether at Twistars, Michigan State, or his home. This time, Larry blocked her mother's view and covered Presley's waist with a towel. Presley had heard whispers about his signature "treatment," but of course she thought it was medical. "I remember thinking as it happened, This is the treatment," Presley says, as he pushed aside her yoga pants. "He didn't say what he was doing or why. He didn't wear gloves. He didn't bother to tell my mom what he was doing. The whole time, I thought my mom knew."

He abused Taylor when she saw him for treatment in the back room of Twistars one evening, after he was done seeing the girls who were members of the gym. "I was alone in the room with him," she says. "I was in a leotard and shorts; he said to take off my leotard and wear my shorts and a T-shirt." She thought it seemed odd that he would ask her to change out of her leotard, but he was the doctor. Then, she says, "He was having a casual conversation with me as he was doing it." She hadn't heard the rumors about the procedure, and afterward, feeling deeply uneasy, she made a beeline for Presley and a few other girls she knew at the gym that night. She told them what had happened and asked what they thought.

They said it was his usual treatment, that he did it to everyone. "I thought, OK, I'm not different," Taylor says. The fact that the doctor did the same thing to everyone helped normalize it in their young minds. It wasn't as if he was targeting anyone individually for anything inappropriate, they thought.

The two girls saw him on occasion for minor things after that— but they made sure never to see him for lower back pain, since that's the excuse he had used for the penetration. He often used back or hip pain as an excuse, although he did the procedure for other kinds of pain as well, such as leg pain, claiming that applying pressure to one part of the body helps another. His chosen "treatment" likely depended on the trust or vulnerability of the patient.

Taylor says there were times when her back pain got "super bad," but regardless, she would not go to Larry for help with it. Even though she and Presley had decided his method must be medical, it made them highly uncomfortable. "I did not want to put myself in that position again," Taylor says.

Presley thinks perhaps they "weren't as brainwashed," she says, because they had left the isolated universe of Twistars, where everyone had to fall in line, and joined their high school team. "We were in it, but also outside of it, looking in," she says. Taylor adds that they had much more autonomy on their high school team than they did at Twistars, noting, for instance, that "we were given time to heal from our injuries."

Looking back, Taylor wrestles with the moment she reasoned that the procedure must have been legitimate. "I knew initially it wasn't normal. I believed in myself. I think that's the hardest part, knowing that if I had just trusted my gut instinct and would've said something . . ." Her voice trails off. Presley reminds her that she was a young girl and he was the respected doctor. Taylor nods. "Still, it's so hard," she says. "You flash back to these memories. It makes you start to question everything, like what else have I missed? It makes you play mind games."

It's painful to see her questioning herself because a predator abused her as a child. I remind her that the abuse is on him, not her, and that there is power in her story: girls who read it will know that they can trust their gut if something seems off with an adult, no matter how famous or "important" that adult may be. It's a powerful message, one that can change lives. But for both young women, more emotional hurdles would come, as they will divulge later.

The two friends' experience serves as a crucial reminder of something we sometimes forget: kids don't think like adults.

In my years of reporting on sexual assault, I once interviewed a woman with key insight into how children think, based on her own experience. Jennifer Fox, the writer and director of the autobiographical HBO film *The Tale*, was thirteen years old when her running coach befriended her and made her feel special, eventually luring her into bed. He was nearly three decades her senior, but she didn't see him as an abuser. Instead, she thought of him as an older boyfriend, her first love, even though he pressured her into sex that was so painful, it made her feel sick. In her kid mind, she was in control of the situation, making her own decisions.

Decades later, when she was in her forties, she looked back on the childhood experience, trying to make sense of it. She wondered why she had allowed herself to get embroiled in such a scenario as a young girl. She had to remind herself that her adolescent brain saw things differently. "We look back with adult eyes," she told me. "The film is much about that. As an adult, I'm asking my young self, How could you have done that? I don't understand why my thirteen-year-old self went ahead with this. But that's because I've now passed over—I'm no longer the same person I was at thirteen."

Another survivor of childhood abuse once gave me key personal insight into how kids think as well. She was a seventh grader at the Horace Mann School, an elite prep school in New York, in the early eighties, when a teacher in his forties offered her a ride home after school, then brought her to his place, offered her a gin and tonic, and raped her. (She asked me to keep her name private but wanted to share her story to help people understand the minds of children.) After the assault, she recalled, "I didn't tell my parents what had happened. Instead, I said I'd had pizza with a friend and had fallen asleep at her house. I know that sounds strange, but a child's brain is not rational. In fact, I remember feeling angry at my mother for failing to protect me."

She also felt ashamed, she told me, noting, "My parents never talked about sex; I thought sex was bad." The teacher raped her several more times that year, and she continued to avoid talking to her parents about it. "I felt that somehow they must know what was happening. And since they weren't doing anything about it, they must be fine with it." Sometimes, when she was acting moody, her mother would ask why. "I once said to her, 'You know why I'm angry at you!' She looked utterly bewildered." Her mom had no idea what was going on. But her young daughter assumed she knew everything.

It's an important thing to keep in mind about the Nassar saga— how kids think. Larry certainly figured out this vulnerability in his young patients.

Chapter Ten

The Club

About ten miles outside of Lansing lurks a monolithic white and light-green building at the end of a long, tree-lined lane in the town of Dimondale. It's a massive complex called the Summit, home to various sports facilities and gyms, including Twistars USA Gymnastics Club.

The road to Twistars is fairly secluded, not much around but trees. I walk along that road on a sunny Friday afternoon, imagining all the girls getting dropped off by their parents here over the years, carpooling with neighbors, or traveling from across the state or even from out of state. Today, there aren't many cars on the road. A bearded man on a Harley rolls up and asks if I know the whereabouts of a landscaping store; I do a search on my phone for him, and he roars off. At the Summit, I'm surprised I can just walk right in the door, no questions asked. And there it is, immediately to my left: Twistars. I park myself on a blue wooden picnic bench in the giant lobby outside the gym. There are kids in the gym, girls in bright leotards lounging around on hefty orange and green mats, apparently awaiting class in the lofty, cavernous room. Some are stretching, their ponytails swinging. I notice that the leotards—or leos, as the girls call them—have gotten much snazzier than the one I wore as a kid. Mine was a subdued navy blue, long sleeves, a white stripe down the sides. Now they're sleeveless, backless, patterned, flowered, fabulous.

More girls wander into the building. "Hey, Soph," calls one. They arrive in T-shirts, jean shorts, and flip-flops, carrying backpacks and gym bags. They stuff their belongings into metal lockers, banging them shut. A vending machine boasts "Fresh Healthy Vending," offering fruit snacks, cashews, Clif bars. No sugary grape soda here. There's an ice rink across the lobby, and a wall lined with retro arcade games—an Indiana Jones pinball machine, a Ms. Pac-Man—along with some more modern offerings. Inside Twistars, I can see a wall lined with medals, photos, and newspaper articles about star gymnasts. A pink sign at the entrance to the gym says, "Fight like a girl."

Indeed, the girls look like fighters—muscular and strong. But vulnerable too.

There was a time when I would have looked at these girls and thought, Wow, how wonderful—future stars of gymnastics. But instead, I get a dark feeling. The predator has left the building, but the place feels haunted. I'm surprised kids are still coming to this gym at all, given its history. John Geddert retired from the gym after USA Gymnastics suspended him in the wake of the Nassar scandal, amid complaints of abusive coaching. In a letter to parents, he said the suspension was based on false allegations. His wife runs the place now.

Just down the road from Twistars, I stop into the Comfort Inn, the same hotel where Lindsey Lemke and her mom used to stay on occasion. The hotel manager tells me she did gymnastics as a kid herself, decades ago. Standing at the front desk on a slow afternoon, she recalls how she trained at Great Lakes Gymnastics, the gym where Larry got his start. She was around ten years old when she fell off the balance beam and landed badly, injuring her tailbone.

"My mom pulled me out," she says. "I was so bummed. I didn't want to quit." But her mother insisted, saying, "It's too much for your body at this age." As a child, she thought her mom was "too overprotective," she says. But when the Nassar scandal flared up, she says, "I thanked God I escaped." As she tells me this, I feel a chill. She got out before the doctor got his hands on her. Still, the devastating news hit close to home: her daughter now has friends who were abused by Larry Nassar.

That day, I meet a young woman who grew up training at Twistars, Valerie Webb, and she tells me about another disturbing aspect of this tale. Larry not only abused her at Twistars and the Michigan State clinic, but at her high school too. Indeed, he served as a physician for students at Holt High School, near his home, and he used a training room at the school as yet another venue for his abuse. Larry's tentacles stretched across the community—and the world.

When I meet up with Valerie in Lansing, she has a gentle, trusting air, a young voice. I can picture her as a child at Twistars, just like the energetic girls I saw at the gym, and I feel that familiar pang. Now in her early twenties, she tells me that she started doing gymnastics when she was four years old, heading to Twistars when she was seven. At the gym, Larry treated her for minor injuries. Then she suffered a major injury, falling from the high bar and fracturing her spine, requiring surgery. When she got back on her feet, her back hurt, and Larry grabbed the chance to take advantage of her.

She was ten years old when she went with her mom to the Michigan State clinic and he abused her for the first time. He told her to put on a pair of shorts, then blocked her mother's view, slipped his hand inside the shorts, and penetrated her, while breezily asking her about family, friends, school. He claimed the "treatment" would spare her from more surgeries. She remembers that the procedure was painful, but he was the renowned doctor. "I never thought he would harm me," she says. "It didn't occur to me to say something." She also thought that since her mom was there, everything must be fine.

When Valerie started attending Holt High School, she saw Larry for the "treatment" at her school. He headed over to the school on Friday nights, she says, to be on hand to treat the football players at the games. While the players were on the field, Larry sometimes arranged to meet Valerie in the football training room, known as the "war room," she says, and abused her there. It seems that he maximized every minute of his time. Over the years, he befriended Valerie, performing thoughtful little gestures like getting her a signature from Olympic medalist Nastia Liukin. And he continued molesting her throughout her teens.

She believed in him so deeply that after the allegations of abuse hit the news, she vehemently defended him, even on a local radio show. She said on the air, "He's an amazing doctor that always tried to help me." But as time passed and she heard the stories of other women who had been abused, she came to realize, "This is exactly what happened to me."

She posted on Facebook: "Me too."

Later, in her victim impact statement in court, she said she had endured seven surgeries to her back, after the doctor had claimed his "treatment" would prevent the need for more operations. "Larry, you brought me close to you so that you could manipulate me for your own good, make me think that you were a good person and doing this to help me. But all along, it was only to help yourself," she said. "Why would a doctor, of all people, not give me the best treatment?" It's a question that haunted her as she came to recognize her doctor as a predator.

That night, after my attempt to get a late dinner at Arby's is thwarted—apparently it's against the rules to walk through a drive-through—I think about Valerie and about the young girls bouncing around Twistars in their festive leotards. They looked so hopeful. So young. So trusting. So eager to please. Such easy prey for a predator.

I think back to my own experience in gymnastics as a kid in Indiana at the Girls Club. I was good at the techniques— handsprings, walkovers—but felt self-conscious doing some of the more dance-y moves that were part of the floor routines. The coach told me to embrace the routine and to really *feel* it, to show the audience how much I cared—because she knew I did care. She was right. I cared deeply. I wanted to impress her, so I followed her advice, striving to truly own the routine. Later, I remembered her words of wisdom when I performed a routine with my friend Jessica onstage at the annual Watermelon Festival in our hometown of Brownstown. We did the routine to a favorite oldie by the Supremes, "Where Did Our Love Go?" I embraced the moves. We had a blast.

Maybe I was lucky that we didn't have a more hard-core gym in my town. After I maxed out the lessons at the Girls Club, I moved on to basketball and tennis, since my school had teams for those sports. I never looked back. The gymnasts who grew up at Twistars during the Nassar years would be fighting demons throughout their lives, looking back and questioning everything. This is what predators do to people.

Chapter Eleven

The Con

Prowling his way through the decade in the 2000s, Larry's manipulation of families grew ever bolder and more diabolical. Isabell Hutchins, or Izzy, as everyone calls her, knows this all too well. She and her parents agree: Larry contributed to the breakup of their family. He also contributed to her training and competing with a broken leg.

Izzy, a fun-loving, self-described "goofy" kid, started gymnastics when she was four years old, when her parents were looking for an outlet for her energy. "She was very, very energetic, jumping all over the furniture," her father, Eric Hutchins, says with a laugh. "As parents, we thought, How do we process this?" Izzy's mother, Lisa Hutchins, agrees. "She oozed energy. She was a maniac," she says. "At age two, she started climbing the fridge and sitting up there—it's where we kept the candy. At age four, she was swinging from the tops of doors. She was so athletic and flexible." She was also a cheerful, outgoing kid, Lisa recalls, describing her happiness as "infectious." Izzy remembers that she used to get in trouble for talking too much in class.

"Gymnastics turned out to be a very good fit for her," Eric says. Izzy quickly rose to the top at the Sunrise Gymnastics Academy in Toledo, near the family's home in Rossford, Ohio, a small city along the Maumee River. When she wasn't at the gym, she was experimenting on the school playground, doing backflips off the swings—sitting in the swing, propelling herself forward, then hoisting her feet over her head and flipping herself out backward. She was tumbling around so often, in fact, her mom says, "I talked to her feet more than her face." Izzy's older brother also did gymnastics, and her younger sister, Ireland, joined in as a toddler too, going to Mommy and Me classes with her mother.

"Those were the good years," says Eric. "The fun years."

When Izzy grew out of the Sunrise gym, her mom started driving her to a club about an hour away from home, Halker's Gold Gymnastics. Izzy outgrew that one too.

In 2009, Izzy was around ten years old when a coach told her that to get to the next level, she should go to Twistars to train with John Geddert, noting that John had helped many gymnasts get full-ride college scholarships. Lisa recalls, "Everyone kind of knew of John because he worked with Jordyn Wieber." Jordyn was not yet an Olympic medalist but was a big name in the gymnastics world. The hitch for Izzy's family: Twistars was a two-hour drive away from their Ohio home.

The family differed on whether to make the trek. Eric supported his kids' ambitions but thought the four-hour round-trip drive to Michigan would be too much, leaving the family with hardly any time to see each other. "It was tough enough with an hour drive each way, followed by a two- or three-hour practice," he says. Eric was just getting started in his career in real estate, and Lisa was home raising the kids. Izzy wanted to go to Twistars, as did Ireland, also a rising star at six years old.

"If you went to Twistars, you knew you were being coached by the best," says Ireland, now a seventeen-year-old high school student who is publicly identifying herself as a survivor for the first time in this book.

The two girls worked on their dad to let them go. Lisa wanted to give her kids every opportunity possible and was willing to do the driving to the gym. She herself had done gymnastics as a kid but didn't have a chance to advance because her family lived too far from an elite gym and couldn't relocate. Both Eric and Lisa wanted the best for their children; they just had different ideas about what was the best. Ultimately, Eric says, "I got outvoted."

Izzy and Ireland started going to Twistars, making the journey with their mom, doing schoolwork in the car.

Suddenly, Izzy says, "gymnastics became a career."

I meet with Izzy and her boyfriend, Cody Igo, at an Italian restaurant in Lansing, where we sit outside for an enormous pasta lunch. The two are a striking pair, both college students in their early twenties, athletic and fit. She's tall with wavy, honey-blond hair; he's dark-eyed and clean cut with a big tattoo on his arm—a Greek quote from King Leonidas of Sparta: "Come and Take Them," a challenge to foes to try to take his weapons. Cody sees it as an expression of the protection of his family and nation, Izzy tells me. He got the tattoo when he joined the Army National Guard, before the Nassar scandal, but indeed, he has helped protect Izzy through her ordeal.

Cody orders a drink, and Izzy jokes that she's the designated driver since she herself is not yet twenty-one. They have driven from Ohio, where they both attend college, to talk with me; Izzy hopes her story will help other children and families recognize the signs of a predator. The two have a sweet, natural ease with each other. They reminisce about how they went to high school together but didn't know each other well back then. Embroiled in the gymnastics world, she had no time to socialize. To Cody, she was a mystery girl. He knew only that she was a gymnast, which he thought was cool. "She was ripped," he recalls with a grin, admitting that he had a crush on her. She smiles. He also remembers that she came to school on crutches.

It's a few months after the court hearings when we meet. Izzy and her family are still reeling from the ordeal, with her father suffering seizures from stress. Izzy tells me that at Twistars, she soon began training six days a week—Monday through Saturday, and twice a day on Tuesdays and Thursdays. On those two days, she arranged with her teachers to miss school, as long as she could keep up with her schoolwork, which she did—another high achiever. "Izzy was very focused," Eric says. "She learned a lot about time management at an early age from gymnastics." In between the two-a-day practices, she would remain at the gym. She and her mom often stayed overnight at a Red Roof Inn near the gym to make it all work. Izzy quickly bonded with gymnast Lindsey Lemke and sometimes stayed at her house.

As for Izzy's mom, "I didn't sleep a lot," Lisa recalls. If she wasn't busy driving, she was packing healthy food for the girls for the trips. "I should have bought stock in Tupperware," she jokes. Eventually Lisa got a job at Twistars, working in the office and also helping to train the preschoolers. She recalls that John Geddert was "nice as pie" to her family in the beginning. "He treated us kindly. He was bending over backward, trying to make sure we stayed. Izzy and Ireland were the new talent." Indeed, they were doing exceedingly well. Izzy was invited to train with the top gymnasts, including Jordyn Wieber, and quickly reached the lofty Level 10.

"We were potentially looking at an Olympic route," Eric says. To be sure, when you see videos of Izzy as a young gymnast, she looks like a superhero, doing breathtaking flips. But all the time spent driving to and from Twistars put stress on the marriage, and Eric tried to figure out how to get the girls closer to home in Ohio. He began talking to John about possibly opening a satellite gym in Toledo and became good friends with him, as well as with Larry.

Soon enough, amid all the intensive training, Izzy pulled a hamstring and injured her pelvic bone. "The tides turned when Izzy got hurt," Lisa recalls. John was not pleased. He sent her to see Larry in the back room of the gym.

At that first appointment, Larry massaged her rear and thigh and then, without warning, slipped his bare fingers under her leotard and penetrated her vagina. He raised her leg during the penetration, saying it would help her stretch. He noted that he would tell John how to stretch her leg this way too, minus the penetration. Shocked and confused, Izzy didn't think she could tell him to stop, because he was an adult, the doctor—the Olympic doctor. She thought he must be trying to help her with the pain. Nonetheless, she felt startled and disturbed, having never experienced anything like that.

Afterward, she asked a fellow gymnast if she thought the procedure was strange, but the girl said no, he did it to her too. As a child, Izzy felt relieved, thinking it must be normal if he did this to other girls too. Just as Presley Allison and Taylor Stevens had thought—he normalized his abuse by doing it to everyone. And the young gymnasts were an isolated bunch. "I didn't even know what sexual abuse or sex was," Izzy says. When she saw Larry again the next day, he did the same thing, and she realized it would happen every time. He said she should see him five days a week until the pain eased up, and so she did, meeting him at Twistars or at the clinic at Michigan State. She recalls, "I saw him more than I saw my own dad."

Larry inserted himself into Izzy's life, giving her little gifts, like Michigan State sports medicine T-shirts and Chinese health balls, the little metal balls that you can rotate in your hand to ease stress. The biggest prize: a box of souvenirs from the 1996 Olympics, when the Olympic mascot was a cartoony character called Izzy. There were Izzy figurines, socks, and bandages—which Larry called "Izzy Band-Aids for Izzy booboos." He sent uplifting little texts and gossiped with her at appointments, talking about John's mood during practice. "Larry would be the good cop to John's bad cop," Izzy says. Larry told her he would protect her and look out for her. "He would talk to me like we were friends, and we were; we were best friends. He was my 'Larry Bear-y' and I was his 'Busy Izzy.'"

Meanwhile, she watched John abuse the girls in his own way, she says. She recalls hearing him furiously order one girl to weigh herself, shouting, "Get on the f—king scale!" She also remembers hearing him say inappropriate things to girls about their bodies, such as telling them they could be models for Victoria's Secret. Other times, she says, the girls were pitted against each other. "If someone messed up in practice, we all paid," she says, explaining that all the girls would be sentenced to extra rope climbs or laps to punish and embarrass the girl who had underperformed.

For young Ireland, the coaching turned negative when she felt nervous about doing backflips on the balance beam. "John threw me backward," Ireland says. "He didn't spot me—he threw me."

*****

Gymnasts from across the decades have told me about incidents like this at Twistars. Amanda Smith, now in her twenties, remembers a particularly insane episode that she endured. When I meet with her in Lansing, I'm immediately struck by her warmth and humor; she greets me with a sunny smile and an easy laugh, then sits down and tells me an atrocious tale. She flew off the uneven bars while learning a new dismount when she was nine years old and landed badly, getting a bloody nose and black eye. Then she got punished for being injured. John sentenced her to sit in the oversplits, extreme splits with her feet propped up on thick foam mats on either side, forcing her body to go deeper than the regular splits. "My nose was gushing blood," she recalls, as she did the oversplits, trying not to cry but failing. Meanwhile, her fellow gymnasts were punished for her mishap as well—sentenced to extra rope climbs. Amanda was ordered to remain in the splits for an hour and a half. At some point, Larry wandered by and said, "Well, it looks like I showed up just in time." He helped her get up, cleaned her face, and comforted her, saying she was a great gymnast and that "John can be an asshole." She appreciated the kindness. She came to see Larry's room at Twistars as a "safe" place, she says. Larry would later cash in on that trust.

Amanda was used to getting yelled at by John—she recalls how he would pull her into the locker room and shout in her face, up so close she could feel his spit. Much of his scariest yelling happened in back rooms, she notes, not out in the open. He treated her this way despite being a family friend. Amanda was good friends with one of John's two daughters, and her family once took a cruise with John's family. John nicknamed Amanda "Shark Bait" on that cruise, she says. He said it would be easier to throw her overboard than to hear other moms complain that she was getting more attention than their kids because she was outperforming them. She didn't especially appreciate the weird nickname, but it stuck.

The final indignity came when she was around thirteen and fell from the beam after one of the coaches failed to spot her, she says, and her mother was there to witness the scene. "I was bawling, and he was screaming at me like I was a grown man," Amanda says. "I locked eyes with my mom. The coach said to her, 'You need to control your crybaby.'" Her outraged mother scooped up her daughter and said, "We're never coming back." John was out of town at a competition at the time. When he got back, he heard what had happened and invited Amanda to return to the gym, she says, but her mom stood her ground, saying her daughter could not be belittled by coaches. John got mad and said, "You're done," Amanda recalls. She never went back. She had been at Twistars since she was eight, after starting gymnastics as a toddler and falling in love with the sport, especially the uneven bars. "You had to pry my hands away from the bars," she says, smiling. "I was *that* kid." She'd begged her parents to send her to Twistars, and they had driven her there—more than a hundred miles from home—before moving closer to the gym. "I went in there like a spitfire, full of energy, full of life," she says. "By the time I left Twistars, I was a ball of anxiety, not in my right mind."

Amanda saw Larry again, after she injured her tailbone from pole vaulting in high school. At her prior appointments, when she was at Twistars, he had massaged her butt, claiming one side was stronger than the other. At this new visit, at the clinic at Michigan

State, he escalated. Going into the appointment, she, like so many other girls, thought of him as a "god," she says, because of his work with Olympians. In his office, he asked if she had a boyfriend and if she was sexually active. Then he said, "We're going to loosen all the muscles up," claiming it was a medical treatment. He warned, "This will be painful." He slipped his hand under her shorts, penetrating her anally and then vaginally. "It hurt so bad, tears were running down my face," she says. Next he had her stand and bend over, claiming he needed to check her "alignment." He pressed his body against hers, feeling up and down her spine. She told him it helped, even though it did not, so she would never have to do it again.

"I wasn't the same person afterward," she says. One night, she confided in her boyfriend about what had happened, and he was upset, saying he thought she was no longer a virgin. "He said, 'Your doctor got to touch you, and I didn't?'" Soon after, they broke up. In the months that followed, she grew depressed, lost her virginity, and began dating older boys. At fifteen, she says, "I stared at a bottle of pills." Fortunately, she says, she went on to meet someone wonderful, a policeman who is now her husband and the father of her two children. All along, she says, Larry stayed in touch on Facebook, liking pictures of her wedding and kids.

When the allegations against him made the news, she scrubbed herself raw in the shower. In her victim impact statement in court, with her policeman husband by her side, she said her final words to Larry, telling him, "My children and my husband have gotten less than my best this past year. I have been moody. I haven't wanted to be touched. The things that make me happy barely made me snap to reality this last year, but that ends today. I may not be an Olympian or a Big Ten athlete, but I have a voice. My voice will be the voice for the voiceless, the ones who were let down by institutions like USAG and MSU, the ones that are too afraid to speak or have not yet come forward. I will not stop speaking until I am heard, until we are heard, and things have changed."

*****

Meanwhile, Izzy Hutchins kept training away, trying to ignore the shouts and insults from John at the gym. But her mother, Lisa, confronted him. When she heard the coach call the girls "brats" and "crybabies," she says, she admonished him to "stop making it personal." As a result, she became a "black sheep" in the gym, she says, not just with John but with parents too. "Some of the parents avoided the ones who spoke up. No one wanted to make it worse for their kids."

In 2011, when Izzy was around twelve years old, she developed a sharp pain in her leg. She went to see Larry at the clinic, where he brought her in the side door after hours. He examined her leg, concluding that nothing was seriously wrong. He taped it up, cleared her to continue practicing and competing, and sent her off with a roll of tape. The pain worsened. "I would see Larry every second that I could, hoping that he could help," she recalls. At the same time, Larry built up his relationship with her parents, making himself available for their calls, texts, and questions and offering to help by not billing their health insurer. He said he understood that costs could get exorbitant since they had out-of-state insurance. As he had done with Lindsey Lemke's family, he said he saw Izzy's potential and wanted her to thrive.

Larry began seeing Izzy in his basement at night after practice— nights she remembers vividly for their strangeness. He would set up the massage table in his makeshift clinic, then start a fire in the fireplace and warm a lotion by the flames. He would massage her aching leg, rubbing a lump that had formed at the site of the pain; then he would work his way up to penetrate her, while she lay on her back or stomach on the table with no underwear. The sessions felt like they took forever, she says. Her mother would be upstairs with Larry's wife and kids or sometimes in the basement, where Larry blocked her line of vision so she had no idea what he was doing.

With a regional competition coming up, Izzy felt desperate to ease the pain in her leg—she knew John expected her to compete—

but the pain would not subside. Feeling stressed and overwhelmed by the pressure to win and, subconsciously, she believes, by the abuse she didn't yet understand, Izzy sought an escape. She found it in a razor blade. She started cutting little slits on her wrists. When she feared that this would be too obvious, she moved to the inside of her ankle. She covered up the marks with her socks. In the summer months, she would cut slits on her hip and hide it with her bikini. She's not sure why she did it, she says, but maybe because it felt like something she could control. No one knew about the cutting. If Larry noticed, he didn't say anything.

Her parents observed that Izzy was becoming quieter and more withdrawn—no longer the cheerful, rambunctious kid—but they thought she was just tired from all the training, says her mother, Lisa. She tortures herself now by replaying those years in her head: "No amount of time will heal and make me forget what I allowed to happen under my watchful eye as a mother." Again, it's what predators do: they make everyone question and blame themselves, when the blame is on the abuser.

Izzy competed at the regionals and had a difficult meet, falling several times, but remarkably, she managed to place high enough to make it to the nationals. John gave her a week off to rest her leg. Back at practice, with her leg still hurting like mad, she tried to perform a floor routine but couldn't complete it. She explained to John that she could barely walk. But since Larry had cleared her to practice and compete, she says, John accused her of faking the injury to get out of training. He called her a "liar" and a "baby," she recalls. Then he took it a step further. He publicly humiliated her by making her perform the routine again—substituting the complex flips in the air for simple somersaults on the ground. "Everyone had to stop and watch while I did the routine with forward rolls," she says. "I was sobbing."

Her sister, Ireland, was there on that dreadful day. "John screamed at her and told everyone to gather around," Ireland recalls. Then he got sarcastic. "He said we all needed to watch Izzy do 'this amazing routine.' I was embarrassed for her. I was so scared for my sister."

Afterward, a distraught Izzy sought refuge in the locker room. John stormed in, she recalls, and yelled, "You can't f—ing do this! Get out of my f—king gym!" He said to never come back.

As Izzy tells her story, her boyfriend, Cody, who went through basic combat training when he joined the Army National Guard, says he has found it surprising to learn how similar the extreme training in gymnastics is to military boot camp.

After the blowup with John, Larry finally advised Izzy to go and get x-rays on her leg. Her mom drove her to the hospital—where doctors found that her leg was broken, from a stress fracture. Yes, broken. She had been training and competing on a broken leg for more than a month. As she tells me this, she pulls out her cell phone and shows me an x-ray of the broken bone. Remarkably, the doctors also found a broken elbow. Two broken bones. Izzy got a cast on her leg and scheduled a surgery for her elbow.

When she told Larry about the broken bones, he apologized for not sending her for x-rays sooner, Izzy says. Lisa recalls that he blamed John—and Izzy herself, claiming that Izzy should have been more vocal, even though Izzy had told him about the pain.

Izzy's parents pressed the doctor about the injuries. Ever the manipulator, Larry told each of them what he thought they wanted to hear. He told Izzy's dad, Eric, that the injuries were serious and that Izzy should try a new sport, perhaps diving. At the same time, he told her mom, Lisa, something different, saying Izzy was fine to keep going in gymnastics and had a bright future in the sport. "He said whatever anyone wanted to hear," Lisa says. "This is where our family started being torn apart. As parents, we were played against each other, at the expense of keeping our girl at a gym where Larry would have access to her. It was the downfall to our family."

Eric agrees, saying, "He would pit Lisa and me against each other, telling her one thing and me another. When I go back and read the texts he sent, it makes me ill to my stomach." Eric was very involved in Izzy's life in gymnastics, even though he wasn't the one driving her back and forth all the time. "I was there, really as much as Lisa; I was in the back room at Twistars," he says. As usual, Larry blocked her father's view during those appointments. Izzy remembers feeling self-conscious, worrying that her dad would see.

Looking back, Lisa says, her family, like so many others, felt honored that Larry made so much time for them. "Larry was a text away," she says. "There was never a time he didn't respond." The advent of text messaging had given Larry a powerful way to stay in the lives of families, securing everyone's trust. He also found creative ways to make the girls feel important, Lisa says; for instance, he would videotape them doing stretching techniques, which he claimed he used for teaching. Now she sees all of that in a different light. "He videotaped my girls. He had videos of him stretching and massaging them," she says. "We thought it was a privilege to see Larry. He was the Olympic doctor. He was sending us to big-name doctors to fix Izzy. What we overlooked was, why were we in this position in the first place? Why didn't our doctor, who saw our daughter almost daily, not figure out her leg was broken, her elbow was broken? As a parent, why couldn't I see what was going on? Instead, I was enamored by a wolf in sheep's clothing. A manipulator who was playing all of us."

"We thought he was Mr. Everything Doctor," Eric says.

"My parents got played," Izzy agrees.

Eric still has some of the texts Larry sent him, and he shares them with me—a rare window into Larry's mind, illustrating how the doctor led parents to believe that he cared. In many of the exchanges, Eric expresses distress at Izzy's injuries, asking for advice and saying he thinks she should quit gymnastics to avoid physical problems later in life. Larry agrees. Lisa didn't keep any texts from those days but says Larry told her the opposite. Eric and Lisa discussed the doctor's conflicting advice at the time, arguing about what to believe.

In one text to Eric about Izzy, Larry said:

I have been saying for a very long time she needs to stop gymnastics and be a diver. This is just my opinion because her elbows are very bad and I [k]new they would only get worse. I will help her as much as possible if she stays in gymnastics because I care about her.

When you know the truth behind that text—that Larry was busy sexually abusing Izzy while telling her dad how much he cared about her—the note is particularly galling. Later, when Eric asked if Izzy should stop training on the bars, Larry said:

I still think she should be a diver and could get a full ride scholarship in diving, be far more successful and her body would feel much better. . . . X

Tragically, Eric thanked him for his help and advice:

Thanks Larry for all you've done. . . . It's so hard watching your ow[n] kid fight for something she loves but not understand the long-term repercussions. . . . As you know I want the best for my kids, but not at all expense.

Larry agreed:

Every time I see her I mention the diving. Eric, Izzy is an amazing lady that EVERYBODY LOVES!!! She is the type of kid that makes everyone feel good and laugh. you should be very proud of her. Larry Nassar.

And from Eric:

> That's why this is so hard, I think she could succeed in just about anything she does. Larry, she walks around now like she's 50. Just imagine what 50 is really going to feel like . . .

Larry replied:

> I do not want to imagine it. She needs to make the decision to change sports . . .

Later, Eric said:

> Again, I want what's best for my kids long term. I know she loves the sport and now colleges are starting to heat up. She's a sophomore so she still has a little time to figure something else out. Swim, track, diving . . .

When Eric asked if Larry had spoken to Izzy about switching to another sport, Larry said:

> We did talk but she is staying with gymnastics. Larry Nassar.

Eric replied:

> If only she knew the long-term mental and physical challenge[s] her body is going to feel. . . . Again, thanks for your help.

In an exchange about various treatments, Larry said:

> I reviewed her stretches and she needs to get her butt stronger still soon so she does not drop down her hip and

torque her shin. . . . I wish she would have been a diver!
Larry Nassar.

And finally, a heartbreaker from Eric:

Thanks again for all you do for her. Tough to watch as a
father, that's for sure. . . . You know me, I like to [err] on
the side of caution. Other people like to get these kids right
back out there. Hence the reason so many girls are broken.
I respect your evaluation/opinion.

Larry spent so much time responding to the family's questions
and concerns, they continued to believe he was a friend who cared
for them. They even went to his house one Saturday after practice to help him when his basement flooded, carrying boxes up
the steps and bringing home scores of his photos from the Olympics, carefully separating them and laying them out to dry in their
house. Just as friends do.

Meanwhile, Ireland steadily moved up through the levels at
Twistars, training with the top girls at the two-a-day practices and
climbing to Level 9. When she began to suffer injuries to her wrist,
ankle, and neck, Larry started abusing her too. Ireland says she
was not as close to him as Izzy, but still, she considered him to be
a friend and confidant. "He was always someone you could talk to
and bad-mouth John, and you knew he wouldn't say anything,"
she says. She didn't talk to anyone about what Larry did to her at
the appointments because she didn't know there was anything to
talk about—he was the trusted doctor. She believed he was performing a medical procedure.

When Izzy recuperated, she wanted to keep training. She had
worked so hard, and for so many years. She and her family had
sacrificed, and a college scholarship loomed. She didn't want to
quit—but she did want to get away from John and Twistars. So in

2012, she started going to a new gym, Splitz Gymnastics Academy, which was about half the distance from home as Twistars. Ireland went too, relieved to get away from the merciless Twistars. In the meantime, their parents separated.

Larry and Izzy stayed in touch on Facebook, with her tagging him in her posts, which he would always take the time to like. Occasionally she saw him for treatment. He gave her a new gift, a big one: an electric nerve stimulation machine to help with pain. Meanwhile, Eric and Lisa were in and out of court, going through the divorce proceedings, making it official in 2014. "It was tough on the family," Eric says. Both he and Lisa agree that Larry and the world of gymnastics were a major factor in their split.

That year, Izzy verbally committed to the University of Arizona for a full-ride scholarship. "This was everything I had worked toward my whole life," she says. Then she tore a ligament in her knee and needed another surgery. She tried to keep going with gymnastics, but a surgeon said that if she did, she would have so many physical problems as an adult, she wouldn't be able to hold her own child if she became a mother. She knew what she had to do, even though the thought of it terrified her. It had been her greatest fear for years, having to leave gymnastics. Her family had spent tens of thousands of dollars on training, surgeries, and rehab. But she had "no love left," she says, for the sport that took so much from her, and "no more motivation to put myself through this." Her mom was upset that Izzy had worked so hard, only to lose her dream. Her father was relieved that she was done.

But something good happened for Izzy too. In her senior year, she began dating her boyfriend, Cody. "He has helped me so much to try to get back to who I would've been," she says, referring to her former bubbly personality, before she became an elite gymnast and withdrew from the outside world. "I was such a crazy energetic child."

In the fall of 2016, Izzy went off to college in Ohio and consulted Larry for his advice on her major. She wanted to study sports medicine, just like him. He advised her to become a physician's assistant so she would have time for family.

Around this time, Ireland decided she was done with gymnastics herself. After more than a decade, the sport had become just a grueling grind. "I told my dad that for my fifteenth birthday, I wanted to quit gymnastics," she says. "That would be my birthday gift."

That fall, the Nassar scandal made the news. At first, the two sisters didn't believe that their trusted doctor's treatment could have been sexual, not medical, as they'll explain later when their story unfolds.

Chapter Twelve

The Final Act

Striding into a new decade in 2010, Larry increasingly used the power of social media and text messages to gain the friendship and trust of the young girls in his care. With Facebook and Instagram, he could enter their bedrooms at night, liking their photos and posts, complimenting their looks, congratulating them on their wins. He was a busy man: he put quite a lot of time into grooming all of his targets, both online and off.

Autumn Blaney was among them. One of the very last survivors in this nearly thirty-year saga, she remembers how special she felt when Larry invited her to text him at any time, even at night, to book appointments. He said he would always make time for her. He told her mom the same: call anytime. He would be there. They thought, How wonderful that this renowned doctor makes himself available to us. Starting when she was around ten years old, Autumn says, "I would always text him, like, every day. I'd text mainly about injuries, but sometimes I would call him if I was going through a hard time. Because I had so many injuries, we had a really good relationship." He had a nickname for her: "Chipmunk."

Autumn is sixteen when I meet with her and her mom, Kris Day, early on a Sunday morning in Lansing. (Well, early for me, not for Autumn, another early riser from her training.) It's a few months after the guilty pleas and victim impact statements in court, and Autumn has just recently decided to speak out. As her mother tells me before we meet, "Autumn has recently and bravely found her voice and wants to use it. She feels she spent time ashamed and hiding and now understands that none of what that monster did to her was her fault." Autumn looks very young and, at the same time, very wise. On first glance, you see a fresh-faced teenager with a cascade of blond hair and sparkling green eyes, summery in a jean skirt and sandals. And then you hear her talk, and it's clear that she is a leader beyond her years. She is brave to share her story with the public. She is doing so to help empower other girls.

Autumn stepped into John Geddert's universe in 2011, when she was nine years old. She had shot to the top of Infinity Gymnastics Academy in Brighton, Michigan, where she had been competing since age five. "I've always been really competitive. Even if I'm just playing volleyball in the backyard, I have to win," she says with a laugh. "In gymnastics, I just remember wanting to train and become really, really good." The logical next step to advance was Twistars. Her mom began driving her there, about a forty-five-minute trip, and later started homeschooling to help her navigate everything. "All of us did things to make it possible," her mom says of the family—her husband, two older kids, grand-parents. "She was that good at it. She was being watched for the 2020 Olympics."

Indeed, at Twistars, John zoomed in on her right away. "I remember the first day I came, he was watching me all the time," Autumn says. "The funny thing is, when you first meet John, he's the nicest person ever." Colleges were watching too, coming to the gym to scout. Autumn smiles as she recalls going home one day as a kid and saying, "What's Yale?" Things got intense, fast. "I remember John being on me all the time. I remember him watching what

I ate. He was always watching me. I was skinny, but he would never let me eat anything. I could eat salad, basically. I would never eat dessert, not even when I was home. I was afraid that John would know. It was always scary." He watched her Facebook page too. Kris recalls posting a shot of Autumn having fun riding a mechanical bull on a family trip. "About five minutes later, I get a text from John, saying, 'Why would you put my Ferrari on a machine like that?'" Kris shakes her head at the thought of it. He had called her daughter a Ferrari.

"When you're involved in that situation, you don't see it until you're out," Kris says. "Why did we put up with these things?" Autumn nods, explaining, "It's like a cult. It's weird, but when you're in it, it's normal. Even things that I questioned, I would just throw into the back of my mind. You're not allowed to question. You get punished. Brainwashed."

Kris kept a close watch over her daughter, accompanying her to Twistars and observing the training from the room above the gym. She couldn't hear what was happening from up there, but if she saw something that made her uncomfortable, she would either text John immediately or talk to him later in his office. "Mom was the only one who ever talked back to him," Autumn says. "She wasn't afraid of him. I was like, 'Mom, please don't. He's going to take it out on me.'" But Kris stood firm.

When Autumn climbed to Level 9, just a notch away from the top level in the Junior Olympic realm, a coach from the Karolyi Ranch saw her competing in the national championships and was impressed. He invited her to attend training camps at the ranch, where she could train with some of the best young gymnasts in the country. Autumn felt honored. The ranch, founded by coach Bela Karolyi and his wife, Martha Karolyi, served as the training center for the US National Team and US Olympic Team. Bela Karolyi had famously coached gymnast Nadia Comaneci to the first perfect score in history. "I thought, Is this real?" Autumn says.

She headed off to the ranch in Texas, and John went with her, as did her mom.

On the road, Autumn was surprised to see John loosen up a bit, even letting her eat pancakes at a restaurant. One night at the ranch, he knocked on her door and left a gift—a pair of stuffed animals, one for her and one for her roommate, a fellow gymnast from Twistars. She found his hot-and-cold behavior confusing. "You go from him yelling at you all the time and then there's this nice guy; it was like multiple different personalities. It was weird. It was like, why?" Autumn says, noting that life at the ranch was extremely stressful. "I was with all these girls I was competing with. You want all the attention on you, so you have to be perfect all the time. It was a lot of pressure that I put on myself. You never get to rest when you're there. You always want to be perfect for the coaches."

She felt reassured that her mom was nearby while she was at the ranch in Texas. Parents were not allowed at the ranch itself. Her mother stayed at a hotel down the road. "I would just call her at night and say, 'Can you just be there when I fall asleep?'" Autumn says. "I would get really homesick because I was there for like five days."

"She and I were just so attached at the hip," Kris says. "We did everything together."

"Everything," the two say in unison, laughing.

Autumn ended up going to training camps at the ranch around a half-dozen times, she says. "I used to sneak food in her suitcase so she'd have snacks because the food at the ranch was horrible," Kris says. "I'd hope that going through security, John wouldn't notice." But he did. "He sent me a long email about following the rules. I shot back and said, 'If she's not taking the snacks, then she's not going.' She's this tiny little girl—she needs to eat. And they were mostly healthy things, protein bars and peanut butter."

There's a poignant photograph from the time, showing Autumn with another Twistars gymnast sitting in the trunk of a car with their suitcases, grinning—a silly snapshot taken as they headed off to the Karolyi Ranch. The girls look tiny, young, excited. I think of Amanda Smith, the gymnast who was sentenced to the oversplits as a punishment for getting injured, and how she entered the sport so full of spirit and left it unable to think straight. Autumn observes, "It's hard to explain what it's like to be a gymnast. It's a very weird sport." Her mom agrees. "It's the perfect storm for predators," she says. "Looking back, it really is the perfect storm."

Autumn met Larry in her first year at Twistars. "I hyperextended my knee," she says. "I was like, I get to meet him? That's Larry Nassar, the Olympic doctor. It was like an honor to meet him." He quickly became her friend. "He would ask you about everything John didn't care about—school, home, friends," she says. In the beginning, when she saw him for minor injuries, he didn't do anything abusive. She thought he was generous and kind. If she saw him for an appointment at his house, he would have muffins and juice waiting for her. "I thought, He's my friend. He's the only one I can talk to badly about John, and he's not gonna say anything."

Autumn had learned, like so many girls before her, that injuries weren't acceptable to John. "Whenever I had an injury, he would just be done with me. I felt like I had to do anything I could not to be injured, to be on his good side. You don't want to be on his bad side; he's like a bully." Once, when she had to wear a boot for a fractured shin, she shed the boot to compete at a meet. "You're so trained to block out pain," she says. Understandably, she had a hard time performing the floor routine with her injured shin, and "John was really unhappy with me," she says. "He wasn't paying attention to me. I didn't want to put the boot back on because I knew he'd be mad at me. You had to do the impossible with John. I look back and say to myself, Why did you do those things? I don't know. You just do it. You have to exceed expectations."

No matter how vigilant her mom was, she had only so many eye-balls, and she couldn't possibly see everything all the time. Autumn recalls a time when John pushed her off the uneven bars. He was mad at her, she says, but she didn't know what she had done wrong. Another time he strolled into the locker room when she was in there with another girl, getting dressed. The other girl told him it was inappropriate, Autumn recalls, noting, "He did not like her." And then there was the time she was learning a new skill on the bars and mistakenly kicked him in the face, setting him off. "He was swear-ing; I almost peed myself because I was afraid he would hurt me."

Another time, he embarrassed her with a sexual question, asking, "Autumn, what's a hoo-ha?" She was jumping on a tram-poline when the question came at her from out of the blue. Flus-tered, she tried to explain that it was slang for a vagina. "I know what it is," he said, snickering. Sometimes he would whistle at her, she says, recalling how he did so when the girls went line danc-ing in Nashville after a meet, making her feel uncomfortable. "I never liked him being around Mom either," she says, noting that her mom, pretty and petite with blond hair like Autumn, seemed to draw his attention.

Autumn didn't mention the bad stuff to her mother because she didn't want her to confront John. "She didn't want me to rip his head off," Kris says. "She knew I had a mouth." Autumn nods, saying that she liked knowing that her mom was there, protecting her; she just didn't want to cause trouble with the coach.

"I remember actually peeing myself one time, with a different coach, not John," Autumn continues. She was practicing on the uneven bars and said she had to go to the bathroom. The coach said not yet. When her abdomen hit a bar, she says, "I peed everywhere. My leo was all wet. My teammates had to clean it up." Her mom wit-nessed that one. "I saw it. I went into John's office and let him have it," Kris says. "The coach that it happened with called me that night and tried to excuse it away, and I pretty much let him have it too."

Meanwhile, John was building his winning reputation around the country and the world. At the same time, his tactics were coming under scrutiny at home. In 2011, Michigan police investigated him for assault and battery after a Twistars employee said he assaulted her in the parking lot outside the gym, according to the *Lansing State Journal*.[9] The woman said he stepped on her foot to stop her from walking away and chest-bumped her during an argument. Prosecutors didn't press charges.

That same year, John was named the USA Gymnastics World Team head coach, according to his LinkedIn page. He was on his way to the top.

Also that year, fifteen-year-old gymnast McKayla Maroney told John about the questionable treatment from Larry, according to an interview she did with *Dateline* after the Nassar scandal.[10] Larry had been abusing her for two years when, one night at the world championships in Tokyo, he took it to a new level, molesting her on a bed while alone with her in a hotel room. "I was bawling, naked on a bed, him on top of me, like fingering me. I thought I was going to die," she told *Dateline*. "It was escalating. I didn't feel like it was him anymore—it was this other thing that took over, the dark part of him."

The next day, in her young mind, she hoped someone would notice the distraught look in her eyes and ask what was wrong. When no one noticed her sadness, she mustered the courage to say something. While riding in a car with other gymnasts and John after a practice, she mentioned the awful night. She told the group, "Last night, it was like Larry was fingering me." She said it loudly, and John didn't react, she told *Dateline*. Larry continued to abuse her for years.

Larry and John moved forward together, heading overseas to London for the Summer Olympics in 2012. John had reached the pinnacle: a head coach for the US Olympic Team. That's the year the US team—Gabby Douglas, McKayla Maroney, Aly Raisman,

Kyla Ross, and Jordyn Wieber—won the team gold. The gymnasts became known as the Fierce Five for their accomplishment and drive. Publicly, they beamed with pride. Privately, they all suffered abuse at the hands of Larry Nassar.

The gymnasts at Twistars watched the Fierce Five soar to Olympic victory from home in Lansing, rooting especially for their friend Jordyn Wieber, the superstar who had trained with them under John at Twistars. The whole town was watching. Lansing attorney Jamie White recalls how he and his wife, Christine, pulled their car over on the roadside to see a livestream video of Jordyn winning the gold.

When Autumn Blaney turned ten, meanwhile, she made it to Level 10, and the training got more punishing. That year, "my hamstring came off the bone," she says. Larry seized the opportunity to add abuse to his routine, which had previously consisted of massaging her body and using acupuncture needles. When the abuse began, her mom was in the room, but Larry cagily blocked her line of vision, as usual. "I remember he put a towel over my butt. I was facing away from my mom. I had my leo on, and he pulled it up to the side. I remember thinking, Ugh, what are you doing. And it just hurt. I always remember, his nails were sharp. That's what I remember. And I had to go to the bathroom after," Autumn says. "He acted like normal. He had his eyes closed, like usual," she says. The doctor often closed his eyes while working on patients. "He didn't say anything to Mom, didn't explain what he was doing, didn't wear gloves. I didn't tell Mom about it. I was embarrassed. I didn't want anyone to know."

I think about how self-conscious girls are about their bodies at this age. I remember being a kid in my leotard in gymnastics class at the Girls Club and worrying that my belly wasn't flat enough. My friend Kelly's stomach was super-flat. Now, when I look at the photos from the time, I can't believe I was concerned about that; I was tiny. But it reminds me of how body-conscious I felt as a young girl. I can picture why girls wouldn't want to talk about embarrassing things that happen in the doctor's office, especially at a time when their bodies are changing.

Larry would go on to abuse Autumn hundreds of times, while pretending to help her and fostering his friendship, bringing gifts from the Olympics—a patch, a pen. But she always dreaded the massage table. "I hated it. It lasted for as long as forty minutes. It was very uncomfortable," she says. "He would say, 'Does that feel better?' And I'd say no. So he'd move and say, 'Does that feel better?' And I'd say yes, just to make it stop. But it never did." She adds, "The one thing that haunts me is that I finally got up the courage to say, 'I don't like this.' He said, 'I know.' And he just kept doing it."

Autumn knew he did the same thing to other girls. "All of us girls would say, 'Does Larry do that to you?' And we would say, 'Yeah.' That's all we would say." Just like gymnasts Presley Allison and Taylor Stevens, the best friends who left Twistars for their high school team, Autumn and her friends thought that since the doctor did it to everyone, it must be normal; he wasn't singling anyone out. Autumn recalls walking into the room when Larry was doing the "treatment" on another girl. She heard the doctor tell the girl, "Ohh, your hoo-ha hair is growing."

Her mother cringes. She trusted the Olympic doctor. "We thought he was our friend. We thought he was an amazing person. He volunteered all the time," she says. "He volunteered in church— what a great guy."

"He did everything for everyone," Autumn says. "And John liked him because he actually let us compete with problems."

Kris notes that Autumn recently went to see a chiropractor, and the doctor very clearly explained everything that he was doing. "He said, 'OK, Autumn, I'm going to move your hair. I'm going to touch your neck.' We left the appointment, and Autumn said, 'Oh, that's how it's supposed to be.'"

The same year Larry started abusing ten-year-old Autumn, she began getting sick of gymnastics. "I was mentally drained already. It was getting to the point where I had to train more. John was focused on me even more: you can't eat this, you can't do that. I thought, I don't want to have to go through this all the time. But I just did." At the same time, she would get mad at herself for thinking this way. She was training now with Olympic medalist Jordyn Wieber. "I thought, If Jordyn can do it, I can do it. My goal was always the Olympics. I wanted to be at the top." The family was heavily investing now too, spending some $30,000 a year on training, trips to meets, and medical expenses, Kris says. Larry offered to help by not billing the family's health insurer for his sessions with Autumn, saying he wanted to see her succeed. It's the same tactic he used with gymnasts Lindsey Lemke, Izzy Hutchins, and many others—another step in his evolution. Families felt grateful for the apparent generosity from the Olympic doctor amid the hefty expenses of the sport.

Autumn sometimes talked to her mom about leaving it all behind. "We had a lot of conversations about it," she says. "It was very, very hard."

"She'd want to quit, then have a really good meet and want to be back in it again," Kris recalls. "It was hard because she was so, so good. I was afraid she would regret it if she left." But Kris left the decision up to her daughter.

Autumn went back and forth over it for two years. When she won competitions and gained John's approval, she would think it was all worth it, especially when he rewarded her, for instance, by bringing her to the Build-a-Bear Workshop. But if the girls got second place, they would pay. "He would yell at us. He would say, 'You're gonna do twenty beam routines because one of you fell.' He said, 'You're gonna do conditioning till you throw up.'" And sometimes, the girls did throw up.

In the meantime, John Geddert faced another investigation for assault and battery from police in Michigan in 2013, after a gymnast accused him of grabbing her arm and stepping on her foot, according to the *Lansing State Journal*.[11] He said he was disciplining her and had grabbed her to make her sit on a bench, according to the *Journal*; prosecutors declined to press charges, ordering counseling for the coach instead.

In 2014, when Autumn was around thirteen, she decided she was done. "I knew I just couldn't do it anymore. I was at the last straw. I was crying every day after practice, having to ice myself. I was miserable."

"At first I thought, OK, she just had a bad day," Kris says. "Then finally it was like nope, she's done—I could see it."

Telling John was incredibly nerve-racking, Autumn says. "I remember sitting down with him and I was so scared. He said, 'Maybe you shouldn't be an elite, just be Level 10.'" In other words, she could stay at her current level and not strive for the US National Team or the Olympics. "I was so afraid of him. I was like, 'That's not it. I just don't want to do it anymore.' He said, 'Fine, then you have to do two more weeks at the gym.' After that, he avoided me at all costs. He treated me like trash. He treated me like I was nothing."

"After like two practices like that, we were done," Kris says. "We never went back."

When she left the sport behind, Autumn says, "The first week was great. I could eat what I wanted."

"She slept all the time," her mom says. Autumn laughs. "Yes, I got the rest that I needed. Then it was like, now what do I do?"

Her days were no longer regimented: practice, study, eat, practice, eat, sleep. She wasn't used to having oodles of free time on her hands. "The whole transition from out of gymnastics was hard. I don't sit around. I thought, What am I doing? I'm not accomplishing anything with my life. What is wrong with me?" She laughs and says, "I was just thirteen. But I was still wired; I remember feeling strange because someone wasn't telling me what to do all the time—I didn't have a routine. At one point I started crying and

Mom said, 'Are you OK? Do you want to go back?' I said, 'No, I'm actually happy for once.'" Autumn just felt relieved to finally let her emotions out, she says. "It was a weight being lifted off my shoulders, because you grew up not being able to feel anything, not being able to show emotion."

Autumn went back to school in the eighth grade. Following several years of homeschooling and the intense training at the gym, it wasn't easy to return to that world. "I was small but built—I was sixty pounds and had an eight-pack. I looked different, and kids made fun of me for it," she says. She felt like an outsider socially, noting, "I felt like the dumbest person alive, even though I still got straight As."

She continued to see Larry for various issues, including recuperating from a shoulder surgery. "Because he manipulated me so much, I still saw him after I quit," she says. Her final appointment with him at the Michigan State clinic, scheduled for September 2016, was mysteriously canceled by the clinic, she says. She didn't yet know it, but he was on his way out—the allegations of abuse were about to hit the news. Those allegations would leave her reeling, as we will see when we return to her story.

*****

In the final hours before Larry was relieved of his duties at the Michigan State clinic, in August 2016, a thirteen-year-old girl named Emma Ann Miller went to see him for an appointment there. She believes she is the very last survivor in the decades-long saga.

I meet with Emma Ann and her mother, Leslie Miller, at the office of their attorney, Andrew Abood, in East Lansing. It's a few months after the guilty pleas and court hearings, and Emma Ann is fifteen years old, the youngest person I talk to for this book. We gather around a table, and she bravely tells me her story. She hopes to help other girls understand and speak out about abuse. She has already done so: after she gave a fierce victim impact statement in court, a classmate pulled her into the bathroom at school one day, confiding that she had been abused by a cousin and hadn't told anyone. Emma Ann told her she could tell her mom—and she did.

With her long brown hair swept aside into a loose braid, Emma Ann tells me how she had grown up thinking of Larry as a father figure. She speaks with the quiet, dreamy grace of a dancer, and in fact she is a dancer. She has been dancing for as long as she can remember—jazz, ballet, contemporary. She grew up taking dance classes near the Michigan State campus and now performs in national competitions around the country—Toledo, Indianapolis, Las Vegas. "And she always gets good grades," her mom says proudly. Emma Ann smiles and rolls her eyes, then tells me she is creating a new dance solo, which she'll perform to the Demi Lovato song "Warrior." She plans to incorporate a teal ribbon, the color of sexual assault awareness.

Ever since Emma Ann was a toddler, her mom, Leslie, went to see doctors, including Larry, at the sports medicine clinic at Michigan State for help with neck and back pain. She would drive there with Emma Ann nestled in a car seat. Larry was always appropriate with Leslie. Notably, he liked to claim that his invasive procedure was his go-to treatment for back pain. But Leslie had back pain, and he didn't do the procedure—she was an adult. When Emma Ann later developed back pain, he did do it—she was a child.

Emma Ann came to know Larry well from waiting for her mom at the clinic over the years. "He was like a family member," she says, noting that her mom is a single mother, so Larry "was like a male figure in my life."

"There's never been a time when she didn't know him," Leslie says.

Larry had cute little nicknames for Emma Ann, calling her "Goofy" or "Goofball" because she would giggle when he tickled her. "I felt special for knowing him. I thought he cared," she says softly. "But he didn't."

Over time, he employed his shrewd skills to keep Emma Ann close, using social media to let her know that he was thinking of her. "He would text me on Facebook a lot and like all my photos on Facebook. He would ask for dance pictures," she says, "or to see my dance costumes." He gave her his signature gifts too, like a pin and T-shirt from the Olympics.

After decades of manipulating girls, Larry had come a long way from the days when he started testing limits with his likely first victim, Sara Teristi, in the eighties. Back then, he had yet to develop his full arsenal—his grooming skills, his techniques at befriending and ensnaring families, his gift-giving tactics. And of course, the world of social media did not yet exist. By the time he got to Emma Ann, his likely last target, he had become a master predator.

"We thought we were special," Emma Ann's mother, Leslie, says. "He made everyone feel special."

Emma Ann was eight years old when Larry began his profound betrayal of her trust, abusing her at the Michigan State clinic while claiming to help her with her back and neck pain. At the appointments, she recalls, he had a routine: "He would start by adjusting my neck. I'd be on my back and he would fix my neck, and he'd have me, like, turn over and he'd fix my back a little bit. Then I'd turn over onto my back and he would always, like, touch my boobs, before I even had boobs. He would go under my shirt. When I started wearing sports bras or actual bras, he'd go under that," she says. "Then I'd turn back over, and that's when it would start. I just remember it really, really hurt." When she says this, an expression of both deep sorrow and anger crosses her mother's face.

Emma Ann remembers feeling uncomfortable with what he did, but she thought her trusted friend would never hurt her on purpose. "I was like, he's my doctor. Also, he's known me all my life. And my mom and him are super-close." She recalls how one time she was wearing her favorite leggings—black and white, from Aéropostale, which she wore constantly—and he handed her a pair of loose shorts, telling her to wear those for the appointment instead. He could slip his hand more easily into the shorts. She remembers that he would ask her, "Is this OK?" Or, "Does this feel better?" She would either say nothing at all or mutter, "Yup," even though it hurt, hoping he would stop. Her tactic never worked; he kept going. "I just wanted it to be over with," she says. "I feel like he knew I was in pain. You could tell by how I was saying it."

Then she tells me something even more heartbreaking. For a couple of her appointments, she tried out a new strategy: wearing extra layers of underwear. In her young mind, she thought the added pairs of underwear would make it harder for him to access her and hurt her. Of course, that didn't work either.

"I was dumb," she says quietly, almost in a whisper.

That statement kills her mother. "No, you were not dumb! Don't say that! You were a kid," she says. "You're still a kid. Please. Do not say you're dumb. You're extremely smart. Look at your grades."

Larry had the complete trust of both mother and daughter. Not only had they known him for years, but they had also seen him rise to stardom in the sports medicine world. Sometimes Leslie was in the room with Emma Ann during her daughter's appointments, but as usual, Larry strategically positioned himself so Leslie couldn't see and also covered Emma Ann's waist with a towel.

It infuriates Leslie that so many people reported the abuse over the years, only to be ignored by authorities. The predator could have been stopped long before he got his hands on her daughter. "People knew," she says. "I still have so much anger. Either anger or sadness. I don't know if anyone will ever understand the depth of it."

"People knew for years," Emma Ann says.

"I'd like to kill him for what he took from her," Leslie says. "I want to visit him in jail; I want to see him—I want to ask him why he did this."

Emma Ann certainly had a few things to say to him in court, which we'll hear soon.

We take a break from the interview; Emma Ann is hungry, and her attorney, Andrew Abood, buys her a favorite snack from a nearby café, a fruit smoothie and a bagel with cream cheese. This case is very personal for Andrew, whose family has been practicing law in Lansing for nearly six decades; he himself is a graduate of Michigan State. We all go for a spin in his car—a shiny red convertible Camaro. The car is made at the General Motors plant right here in Lansing, he points out.

In the backseat with me, Emma Ann chews her bagel and muses about possibly writing a book one day. Leslie, in the front seat, turns around to show me a video on her cell phone—a powerful moment from Emma Ann's impassioned victim impact statement in court. "Mom, not now!" Emma Ann implores. Our hair is flying in the wind. Emma Ann, at fifteen, looks young and, momentarily, carefree, smiling as we zip along the road, past the fraternity and sorority houses of Michigan State. I think about her mom's chilling words: "what he took from her."

I wonder, how do you trust anyone after such a betrayal, especially when it happens at such a young age? I don't know. But one thing is clear: Emma Ann is a courageous young leader.

Sadly, she could have been spared. While both she and teen gymnast Autumn Blaney were in the midst of their abuse, a young woman named Amanda Thomashow was busy reporting the abuser. She blew the whistle on Larry in 2014, telling officials at Michigan State as well as the police.

What happened next was surreal.

Chapter Thirteen

An Epic Fail

The day twenty-four-year-old Amanda Thomashow walked into the sports medicine clinic at Michigan State to see Larry Nassar, she was wowed by the array of photos on the wall. A lineup of the best and most famous gymnasts in the world. Olympic athletes. Young girls in flashy leotards with big smiles and gold medals around their necks. Larry had treated these phenomenal athletes. And now, he would be treating Amanda. She felt honored. A recent graduate of Michigan State, she was suffering pain from old high school cheerleading injuries. By the time she left the clinic that day, she would look at those photos on the wall once again—and this time, she would see them in an entirely different light. Larry had just molested her, and she knew it. She realized, with horror and certainty, that he had done the same thing to all the girls in the pictures. She knew in that moment, she says: "Those girls were his trophies."

I meet with Amanda late one afternoon at a coffee shop in Lansing, a few months after the court hearings. Sitting down across from me with a glass of juice, she has a relaxed, friendly vibe, looking cool in her asymmetrical haircut, dangly earrings, and faded red jeans. Then she tells me her beyond-outrageous tale. She went to see Larry in March 2014 for pain in her hip. Her mother, a pediatrician who knew Larry, had recommended that Amanda see him.

Larry treated people across the Lansing community, in addition to the gymnasts. When the appointment began, a female resident was in the room, Amanda says, but later, Larry sent the resident away. He first examined Amanda's feet, resting one of them on his thigh, "close to his crotch," she says. He said her problems might be stemming from her foot. He asked her to stand up and bend over in front of him.

When Amanda mentioned a stitch in her shoulder, he told her to lie on her side on the massage table. He slipped his hand under her shirt and massaged her shoulder, then started massaging one of her breasts. Startled, she said, "That's not helping. That's not what I'm here for." He didn't immediately stop. So she said it again. Stunned by his actions, she first thought that perhaps she was "misreading things," she says. She tried to give him the benefit of the doubt since she didn't know much about osteopathic treatments. And she had thought so highly of him.

He sent her for x-rays on her hip and waited for her to return. Then he had her lie facedown on the table. He grabbed some lotion, pushed her shirt up to her bra strap, and pushed her pants down to the top of her butt. He massaged her hips on top of her pants and then, without explaining what he was doing, put his bare hands inside her underwear, cupping her butt. Next he moved on to massage her vagina. Alone in the room with him now, shocked and trying to process what was happening, she suddenly wondered if his patients ever got physically aroused, because the treatment felt more "like something your boyfriend would do," she says. He was on the verge of inserting a finger in her vagina when she said, "Stop." Again, he did not stop right away. So she physically pushed his hand away.

He retreated to the corner and stood with his back to her, she says, because he was sexually aroused.

"Then he used some hand sanitizer and sat down like nothing happened," she recalls. He didn't wash his hands with soap and water, and she wondered if he'd washed his hands after seeing the last patient. He tried to schedule another visit with her, right there in the room, saying, "I'd like to see you before I leave town," she says. She didn't want to make another appointment, but he insisted. When his computer froze and he got frustrated, she told him she would give him a call to schedule the visit. "But he was doing everything he could to get me to stay and make a new appointment," she says. She finally scheduled one so she could escape, knowing she would never return. The doctor said she should tell her boyfriend to give her better massages. He also told her not to worry if she happened to have her period during the next appointment. He said they could work around that.

She fled.

Afterward, she talked to her therapist, family, and friends about the disturbing experience. She called the clinic to cancel her next appointment, explaining that she felt violated by the doctor. The receptionist brushed her off, saying she would cancel the visit because it was "no longer needed," Amanda says, noting that she found the dismissive behavior irritating. She knew she needed to report the incident to authorities. But it was anxiety inducing. "I thought, Oh my gosh, no one's going to believe me. Larry's the good guy, everybody's friend. Everybody loves him," she says. "But the pictures on the wall just kept coming back to me—the little girls in their leotards, his trophies." She began having nightmares. "I'd be running through a tunnel being chased, holding babies."

Amanda reported the abuse in April 2014 to a physician at the Michigan State clinic, Dr. Jeffrey Kovan. He said he would tell officials at the university. Later that day, he called Amanda to say he had done so. Weeks passed with no further word, and she felt increasingly on edge, wondering if her report would indeed go any further. "I had so much anxiety," she says. Finally, in late May, she heard from the Michigan State Office for Inclusion and Intercultural Initiatives, a group tasked with fostering an inclusive campus.

She sat down for an interview with Kristine Moore from that office, as well as with Valerie O'Brien, a detective with the Michigan State University Police Department, which handles criminal matters on campus. Amanda told them Larry Nassar had sexually assaulted her, detailing what had happened at the appointment. She said he had massaged her breast and vagina in a sexual way, that she had pushed away his hand when he tried to insert his finger, and that he had become aroused.

Detective O'Brien then interviewed the accused doctor. Just as he had done with the police a decade earlier, he claimed the treatment was medical and said he touched Amanda on purpose. "I do this on a regular basis. This is a treatment that I lecture on, not only at MSU, but to national and international organizations," he said, according to the police report. "There is no question I was touching her in her private areas. This is what I do." He continued, "I do a lot of hands-on. In her situation, I am beating myself up: How did I not know she was uncomfortable? What signs was I missing? What did I not feel or perceive? I didn't sense anything like that."

And then, he made this strange observation: "Maybe I was just talking too much. She is the daughter of a person I know very well, and I may have been trying to impress her mom. I know her younger sister, who is a gymnast, and her mom is a doctor."

It got weirder from there. "I am known for this. The dean could pick any doctor at the university to work on his wife's rear end and body, and he picked me," he said. He claimed he was in "constant communication" with Amanda during the appointment and that he thought he was making her feel better. Then he claimed Amanda had a "psych history" and that her mom was "too involved" in her life. "So much of it is more mental injury than physical injury," he said. He rambled on, noting that he had liked a picture of Amanda and her sister on her sister's Instagram page following the appointment in question. He said maybe Amanda was mad because she felt that he was "stalking" her, "trying to get into her space too much."

He claimed that's not what he was doing and that he couldn't even remember Amanda's first name.

He told Detective O'Brien he could show her a few videos of his technique. "I can fix their rib by touching their bottom," he said of his patients. He showed the detective some videos, demonstrating his procedure, which he performed on a patient. He said the patient's parents were in the room at the time and that they had recorded the procedure. He said he always asks patients during the treatment, "Does it hurt now? Does it hurt now?" Then he said, "I get her in a position where it doesn't hurt and the pain goes away."

He went on and on. He tossed around medical jargon. He admitted that he got "pretty graphic" in the videos. He called himself the "body whisperer." He noted that during the appointments, "most of the time, my eyes are closed," adding, mysteriously, "use the force; you feel it." He said he gained the trust of his patients, making the point that he performed his treatment on young girls: "I am doing this on ten- and eleven-year-olds." He said he felt "like crap" that a patient thought he had done something inappropriate. "I feel like this little deviant. That is not right."

And, oddly, he mentioned sex with his wife: "My wife, we didn't even have sex until our honeymoon. That is the essence of who I am."

When the detective asked him to describe exactly what happened at the appointment with Amanda Thomashow, he declined. "I don't want to start distorting the memory. I don't want it to be used against me because I can't remember. I could have been distracted and thought I explained things," he said. "I don't want to hallucinate and try to reconstruct it." But earlier in the interview, he had insisted that he explained everything to Amanda—he said he had been in "constant communication."

After the interview, Larry fired off a series of emails to the detective, providing more information about his technique, noting that he had given lectures to Olympic medical staff members. He also provided a Dropbox link to a number of PowerPoint presentations about his method. He even suggested that he demonstrate his procedure on a police officer.

Apparently no one took him up on that offer.

Meanwhile, the Office for Inclusion at Michigan State issued a report concluding that the doctor's behavior with Amanda was "medically appropriate." The university was responsible for investigating the case under Title IX, the federal law that prohibits educational institutions from discriminating on the basis of sex. In its report, the school did not interview any outside medical experts about Larry's technique but instead talked to four of the doctor's longtime colleagues and friends at Michigan State—three fellow doctors and an athletic trainer.

The university's Title IX report, issued in 2014, was later found to be severely flawed. When the Michigan attorney general launched his investigation of the school after the Nassar sentencing in 2018, the investigators slammed the school. Not only did the university fail to interview outside doctors for the Title IX report, but it failed to accurately convey Amanda's allegations to the internal doctors, investigators found. For instance, the doctors weren't told that Larry had massaged her vagina with his fingers in a sexual way, nearly inserting a finger, before she pushed his hand away. "After subsequently learning the details of Nassar's misconduct, each doctor has since retreated from her original opinion," the investigators found.

The investigation also squashed Larry's claim that his treatment was legitimate, citing a former president of the American Academy of Osteopathy. The expert told investigators that contrary to Larry's practice, "intravaginal treatment should typically be utilized only if a patient presents with a trauma-induced history of infertility, irregular menstruation, incontinence, or pelvic pain— and only after external treatment is ineffective." When a physician performs such a sensitive procedure, "clear and informed consent is paramount." If the patient is not of legal age, "informed consent from the patient's parent or legal guardian is required. And when conducting intravaginal treatment on a patient of the opposite sex, a chaperone is standard procedure."

At the time Amanda learned the results of the Title IX investigation, in the summer of 2014, she knew nothing of its substantial flaws. Kristine Moore from the Office for Inclusion called her in for a follow-up and stated that Larry had not violated the school's sexual harassment policy. "She told me they had talked to four female medical professionals and that this is a legit treatment," Amanda says. "She said, 'I'm sorry, there's nothing more I can do.' She kept saying, 'I'm sorry.'" Amanda did not know then that the medical experts were longtime colleagues and friends of the doctor or that they hadn't been told the full story.

When Amanda saw a copy of the Title IX report, she flipped through a few pages and felt her blood boiling. She saw immediately that the document had omitted key details. "They left out that I had to physically push him off me," she says. "They left out that he had a boner." She stopped reading.

Kristine Moore, who is now the assistant general counsel at Michigan State, did not respond to my interview requests for this book.

The university cleared Larry to continue working at the clinic, while establishing some new protocols: he would need to have an assistant in the room when seeing patients, he would need to use little or no skin contact, and he would need to explain his treatment in detail to patients. And so, he continued to see patients, even while the Michigan State Police investigation remained open for more than a year to come, according to the *Lansing State Journal*.[12] And he did not follow the new protocols.

Amanda felt confused, angry, and embarrassed about being dismissed. On the one hand, she says, "I felt that what he did was wrong," but also, she thought, if experts said it was a legitimate treatment, "maybe I was just hypersensitive." Again, she didn't know yet that the experts had close ties to Larry and that they hadn't been given the full picture. Also, she says, "Why would I question the school that I loved and trusted?"

With its lush green lawns and tree-lined paths, the campus had always been a peaceful place, an oasis. Michigan State is also the beating heart of the Lansing community. "The relationship between the community, business, and the university—it's one big blood line," says Jamie White, the local attorney who went to both college and law school at Michigan State, later becoming a key player in the Nassar case. Amanda Thomashow had taken on a giant.

In the summer of 2015, the Michigan State Police forwarded the police report on Amanda's case to the Ingham County Prosecutor's Office. In the police report, Detective Valerie O'Brien noted that an assistant prosecutor had recommended interviewing a medical expert outside of Michigan State. There is no evidence that Detective O'Brien ever consulted an outside expert, according to the 2018 investigation launched by the Michigan attorney general.

The prosecutors who received the police report from Detective O'Brien in 2015 ultimately declined to file charges in the case.

Valerie O'Brien, who is now the assistant chief of the Michigan State Police Field Services Bureau, did not respond to my interview requests for this book.

In further stunning news, it emerged in 2018 that Michigan State had issued two different Title IX reports on Amanda's case in 2014—one version for Amanda, and a secret version for university officials. Amanda's lawyer, Jim Graves, hands me a copy of the two reports when I stop by his office in Lansing.

In Amanda's version, the report ends this way: "We cannot find that the conduct was of a sexual nature. Thus, it did not violate the Sexual Harassment Policy. However, we find the claim helpful in that it allows us to examine certain practices at the MSU Sports Medicine Clinic."

The other, clandestine version ends quite differently, hiding key conclusions from Amanda. This version says the university could be potentially liable for the doctor's actions, noting that Amanda had exposed "significant problems" at the clinic. "We find that whether medically sound or not, the failure to adequately explain procedures such as these invasive, sensitive procedures is opening the practice up to liability and is exposing patients to unnecessary trauma, based on the possibility of perceived inappropriate sexual misconduct. In addition, we find that the failure to obtain consent from patients prior to the procedure is likewise exposing the practice to liability. If procedures can be performed skin-on-skin or over clothes in the breast or pelvic floor area, it would seem patients should have the choice between the two. Having a resident, nurse, or someone in the room during a sensitive procedure protects doctors and provides patients with peace of mind."

None of that was included in the version of the report that Amanda received.

After Amanda was silenced, in 2014, two emotional years followed. She questioned herself, the creepy appointment with the doctor, and the integrity of her alma mater. Her mind swirled with conflicting emotions. "I was questioning myself all the time." Sometimes, she says, "I felt stupid and embarrassed. I doubted myself." She broke off a tumultuous relationship with an unsupportive boyfriend. She retreated from social activities. "I didn't want to be around men, especially men in authority," she says. "I couldn't go to a doctor." The nightmares continued. She tried to regain her equilibrium and move forward, but it was a constant psychological battle.

In the meantime, Larry continued to work at the Michigan State clinic without following the new protocols. He didn't explain the procedure to patients, didn't use gloves, and continued to see patients—including teen gymnast Autumn Blaney and teen dancer Emma Ann Miller—with no assistant in the room. No one ensured that he was following the new rules, including his boss, Dr. William Strampel, then the dean of Michigan State's College of Osteopathic Medicine.

Later, in 2018, after the Nassar sentencing, police charged Dr. Strampel with willful neglect of duty for not enforcing the protocols. Police also charged him with misconduct in office and criminal sexual conduct. He has been accused of preying on young women, allegedly sexually harassing, assaulting, and propositioning medical students at Michigan State. He has pleaded not guilty. An attorney for Dr. Strampel did not respond to my interview requests for this book.

Meanwhile, Michigan State president Lou Anna K. Simon, who resigned under pressure after the Nassar sentencing in 2018, was charged with lying to police about how much she allegedly knew about the Title IX investigation and the accused doctor. She has pleaded not guilty. Her attorney did not respond to my interview requests for this book.

Amanda Thomashow's attorney, Jim Graves, points out that Michigan State has never reopened—or remedied—that flawed Title IX investigation. "The depth of the failure on the part of a Big Ten school is stunning," he tells me. "The reason to conduct an investigation is to get to the truth."

Attorney Jamie White notes that when the two versions of the Title IX report made the news, "the tides turned" in the Lansing community. Many people had believed that the abuse was just an oversight at Michigan State, not a cover-up. "A shoe dropped for a lot of people at that time. It wasn't about an oversight—this was the university making a calculated decision to give the victim one report and the staff a different report." People went from "gathering around the wagon," he says, to calling for accountability and new leadership at Michigan State.

Amanda Thomashow, meanwhile, would go on to become an outspoken advocate for women, which we'll soon see.

Another opportunity to stop the doctor arose in the summer of 2015. US National Team member Maggie Nichols was discussing Larry's disturbing "treatment" with her teammate Aly Raisman at the Karolyi Ranch, and Maggie's coach overheard. The coach was alarmed. "After hearing our conversation, she asked me more questions about it and said, 'It doesn't seem right; it doesn't seem right at all,'" Maggie said in her victim impact statement. Maggie told her coach about the invasive procedure and also showed her some Facebook notes from Larry, complimenting her looks. "My coach thought it was very, very wrong, so she did the right thing and reported it immediately to USA Gymnastics," Maggie said in her statement. "USA Gymnastics and the United States Olympic Committee did not provide a safe environment for me and my teammates and friends to train. We were subjected to Dr. Larry Nassar at every National Team training camp, which occurred monthly at the Karolyi Ranch."

When Maggie's coach reported the doctor to USA Gymnastics in June 2015, the organization started an investigation and suspended him. But the group helped him cover up the reason for the suspension, misleading gymnasts by falsely claiming that he would be absent from sporting events due to personal reasons, according to an independent investigation commissioned by the board of directors of the US Olympic Committee after the Nassar sentencing in 2018. USA Gymnastics then delayed reporting the allegations to the FBI for more than a month, according to the investigation. In addition, USA Gymnastics failed to alert other institutions where the doctor treated patients, including Michigan State, Twistars, and Holt High School. He continued his abuse at these sites for more than a year, until the *Indianapolis Star* ran the allegations against him in the fall of 2016.

The US Olympic Committee failed profoundly as well. The chief executive, Scott Blackmun, and chief of sport performance, Alan Ashley, learned of the allegations from the president of USA Gymnastics, Steve Penny, in July 2015, but the two executives failed to take any action until the *Star* report in the fall of 2016, according to the investigation. Both men are now out at the Olympic Committee. Steve Penny is out at USA Gymnastics as well. As of this writing, he faces criminal charges for tampering with evidence in the Nassar case, allegedly ordering the removal of documents from the Karolyi Ranch. He has pleaded not guilty. His lawyer did not reply to my requests for comment on the allegations.

To be sure, the failures at USA Gymnastics and the US Olympic Committee "extended beyond weak structural elements, governance deficiencies, and failures of oversight," the independent investigation found, emphasizing that both groups "maintained secrecy regarding the Nassar allegations and focused on controlling the flow of information." The failure of the two groups to protect gymnasts was "perhaps best exemplified by the conditions and lack of oversight at the Karolyi Ranch," according to the investigation. Noting that the ranch was the longtime epicenter of training for the National Team and Olympic Team, investigators said, "No institution or individual took any meaningful steps to ensure that appropriate safety measures were in place."

The ranch has since closed, and police are investigating the Nassar abuse that occurred there. Some gymnasts have accused the Karolyis of creating a toxic training environment and failing to protect them. The Karolyis have denied the accusations and have said they did not know of the Nassar abuse.[13] Prosecutors have cleared the Karolyis of criminal conduct, saying there was "no corroborated evidence of any criminal conduct."

I sought comment from USA Gymnastics about its handling of the Nassar case but did not receive a reply. I also contacted the US Olympic Committee for comment, and a representative sent me a response from chief executive Sarah Hirshland. She said the organization today is "very different" from what it was in the past and that it is making necessary changes "to create safe environments, empower athletes, and provide the funding and services our athletes need to perform at the highest level." She said the group has strengthened "athlete safeguards," has instituted "new leadership and stronger accountability measures," and has increased funding to the US Center for SafeSport, the group tasked with combating abuse.

I asked if the US Olympic Committee could pass along my requests for comment to former executives Scott Blackmun and Alan Ashley and was told that the group couldn't help with that.

Larry Nassar, meanwhile, was allowed to leave USA Gymnastics with his reputation fully intact. In September 2015, he announced his "retirement" from the organization on Facebook.[14] In the lengthy post about his career, he bragged about the care he had taken with young athletes over the years, saying his goal was always "to do what is best for the gymnasts." He listed various awards he had won and congratulated himself for helping change "the culture of gymnastics" through his dedication to the girls' health and fitness. He observed, "Overall I hope I have been able to make a good contribution to the sport of gymnastics."

While he "retired" from USA Gymnastics, he continued abusing girls at the other places where he worked or volunteered, including the Michigan State clinic, Twistars, and Holt High School. The FBI, meanwhile, languished, taking at least nine months to formally open a case, according to the *Wall Street Journal*.[15] All while more girls got molested.

In August 2016, the *Indianapolis Star* ran its exposé on USA Gymnastics, reporting that the organization had mishandled reports of abuse against its coaches. That's when former gymnast Rachael Denhollander contacted the paper and named Larry as an abuser, as did Olympic medalist Jamie Dantzscher and National Team member Jessica Howard.

Larry was about to get caught.

Chapter Fourteen

The Board

Jessica Howard felt nervous making that key call to the *Indianapolis Star*. A three-time national champion, she had gone on to serve as a board member of USA Gymnastics. She worried that if she angered officials at the organization by calling the newspaper, "they would destroy me," she says. But pieces from her past were starting to come together. She could see how the abusive sport of her childhood was derailing her adult life. She knew she needed to take action.

Jessica's twisted path to the board of USA Gymnastics sheds light on the misguided priorities among officials and others at the highest levels of the sport, where winning is everything.

We meet in her first-floor Manhattan apartment on a late summer afternoon, around six months after the court hearings, and she sits on the sofa with a Diet Coke in hand, her new pointy-eared puppy, Thor, racing around the room. With a string of festive lights overhead and a calming trio of candles flickering on a glass coffee table, she launches into her story of entering the Twilight Zone. Her life in gymnastics began in Jacksonville, Florida, in 1987, when she was three years old and wore a pink leotard adorned with poodles. When she was seven, she says, she switched to ballet from gymnastics after breaking her ankle twice. But eventually she missed gymnastics. A coach recommended that she try rhythmic gymnastics, a form of the sport that combines gymnastics with ballet, requiring extreme flexibility and strength, incorporating artistic items such as a ball, ribbon, or hoop. She gave it a shot. "As soon as I started it, I was dedicated," she says. "I thought it was magical." She began homeschooling and devoted herself to training. She quickly advanced, and when she was twelve, she moved on to one of the most respected coaches in the sport.

"The first day I went to the new gym, it was a different universe," Jessica says. The coach didn't pay much attention to her that day but showed her how to do a graceful toss with a ball, extending her arm and touching the ball lightly with her fingertips, letting it roll into her hand. "I was enamored with the specificity," she says. The coach said to do the move twenty times. Jessica wanted to impress her. "I could see from the instant I stepped into the gym that she held my dream in her hands," she says. Jessica did the move hundreds of times over the next two hours, trying to get it just right. She didn't even stop for a drink of water. The coach noticed her perfectionist drive and started paying attention. "She saw that part of my personality," Jessica says. "She saw that I could be controlled." The next day, Jessica felt sick after having repeated the move so many times in the hot gym, but still, she says, "I was so in love with everything. To me, the gymnasts looked like Rodin sculptures. I could see the potential. I wanted to be the best I could be." Swooping her little dog up into her lap, she says, "It wasn't about medals, but about fulfilling my potential. Things were serious now. It became a whole mind–body commitment."

She set a goal of getting to the 2000 Olympics. She switched to online school and began training six days a week, five hours a day, in the blazing hot, windowless gym with no air conditioning. "There were days when you would be so drenched, so weak and light-headed, you'd feel like you couldn't walk," she says. On the drive to the gym each day, she would check the temperature on a big sign atop a football stadium. "If it was one degree hotter or cooler, I would register that," she says. But she remained unde- terred. Her coach alternately yelled at her and gave her the silent treatment—which was actually worse. In training, repetition ruled. "There was a list of certain things we had to do to 'pass' the practice—she'd keep you on that thing until you could do it." That could get extremely stressful, for both mind and body. "Your bal- ance gets worse and worse—you could feel it. You know it's get- ting worse, and she's getting angrier and more silent. It was like a complete mental and physical trap. Your body falls over, does wild things. Some days we'd spend a whole day trying one thing, until she kicked us out." One day, she says, she had to repeat the same leap nonstop for two hours. "Repetition is important in terms of training," she acknowledges. "You practice so much, you never make a mistake." However, she says, "It crossed a line."

The sport took over Jessica's being. "My eating habits changed. I barely ate breakfast, or dinner, and ate just a little lunch, maybe a salad with no dressing. I had no interest in food. I didn't feel hungry. I turned myself into a machine," she says, noting, "I was technically anorexic." As much as she wanted to excel, she soon felt a sense of dread on the way to practice. "I had to mentally prepare myself for the hours in the gym," she says. "Sometimes I would be sobbing on my way there." On her thirteenth birthday, she felt confused when her coach gave her a pink, glittery card, then barked that she would not be getting special treatment just because it was her birthday. Her parents told her she could quit, but she didn't see that as an option. She was chasing her dream. She was becoming "an art form," she says. She was the one push- ing herself, and she couldn't stop. "I transformed myself," she says. "I became a sculpture."

She made the Junior National Team, then won a gold medal at the Junior Pan American Games. And, like so many top gym- nasts before her, the more she achieved, the more negative the coaching became. She says she got belittled and berated, with her coach yelling, "You're never going to be anything! You're an embarrassment!" Sometimes the girls were told they looked like "fat elephants" or "ugly sacks of potatoes." For Jessica, the competitions became all about trying to please her hard-driving coach, not about winning. "I don't think I ever heard the words 'good job' or saw a smile," she says. The most she could hope for was a slight shake of the head that indicated she did well enough. She strived for that vague shake of the head. "I was working like a crazy person. People said I looked like the European ideal of a rhythmic gymnast, like a Russian or Bulgarian. That was a big compliment," she says, as the sport has its roots in Europe. "The pressure was extraordinary. I tried not to think of every competition as life or death, dream or no dream." In photos from the time, with her body flexed in impossible, artistic poses, indeed, she became a sculpture.

But she was beginning to crack. The practices were so relentlessly repetitive that the actual competitions started to feel "like a vacation," she says. She suffered pain in her hips, and it hurt to walk. She developed obsessive-compulsive tendencies, picking at her thumbs until they bled and stung. At night in bed, she would run obsessively through her routines in her mind; if she slipped up and forgot part of a routine, she would start over from the very beginning. "I wouldn't let myself get to sleep unless I got through the routine with no mistakes." In 1999, when she was fifteen, she won her first of three national championship titles. The 2000 Olympics were in sight. "But I wasn't happy at all," she recalls. She was descending into darkness. The obsessive-compulsive behavior was progressing. "A good chunk of the sides of my thumbs were gone." Her father noticed her bloody fingers and said she should stop picking. Despite her unhappiness, "I was terrified of letting up," she says. "My mind was wrapped up in maintaining that level, in managing my coach, managing my pain." The obsessive-compulsive disorder entered a new phase: "Going to the bathroom became insane," she says, as she would have to wash her hands or touch the stall door an ever-growing number of times. When her coach "eviscerated" her at a less-than-perfect performance at a practice for the world championships, she says, she thought about killing herself. "I remember feeling like an ant. I felt so small," she says. "To have the power to crush your athlete is an extraordinary power. It's devastating."

A look of pain crosses Jessica's face at the memory. She pauses and tosses a sock ball for her rambunctious puppy to fetch. We decide to resume another day. In fact, we met several times at her apartment over the course of a few weeks to talk about her experience. For Jessica, reliving her past was an understandably emotional minefield. It took time.

Back in her apartment, with her puppy, Thor, banished to the bathroom for jumping all over us on the couch, Jessica resumes her story, telling me that after enduring all the backbreaking years of training, she missed qualifying for the 2000 Olympic Team by a miniscule fraction of a point, per the judging system at the time. She became an Olympic alternate instead. But surprisingly, she didn't feel crushed—she was just trying to survive. Mentally and physically fried by now, she says, "I didn't process it. I didn't even comprehend it. I didn't realize it was a death blow." She just kept going like a machine, always trying to please her coach but never feeling she could. She thought maybe she could make it to the 2004 Olympics. She chalked up more wins.

And eventually, her journey took her to Larry Nassar. As her hip pain progressed, officials at USA Gymnastics sent her to the Karolyi Ranch in Texas for a week to see him when he would be there. She knew he was a big deal, and she felt proud. "I thought it meant I was important to these people," she says. "I was one of the people to be taken care of." The ranch turned out to be a horror, even though she got to escape her ferocious coach. Jessica was at the ranch solely to see the doctor, not to train, and she felt isolated and alone, especially since no parents were allowed at the ranch. "The ranch was in the middle of nowhere," she says. "It was like a prison on an island where you couldn't escape." She stretched by herself during the day and slept on a bunk bed in a cabin with roommates at night.

When she first met Larry, she recalls, "I didn't find him scary at all. Nothing about him raised a red flag or seemed aggressive. And I thought of myself as being perceptive." She notes, "He had the full support of USAG—I trusted him." At her first appointment, he asked her to take off her underwear and put on a pair of loose shorts. She did so and got on the table. He abused her immediately, without telling her what he was doing. She was at the ranch alone, in the room alone—easy prey. "I was in the perfect place to be abused," she says. "He could see it the second I walked in the room." With her hip pain threatening to end her career, she desperately needed his help. "It was an all-or-nothing week. If I couldn't stop the hip pain, I knew this could end," she says. "I still wanted to fulfill my potential, to be that piece of art that I dreamed of."

Recalling her week with Larry, she says, "I see these very clear images—him standing over me, the proximity, the helplessness of being on the table, the rigidity of my body, lying on my back. His glasses. His greasy hair. A bookshelf in the room. A hanging TV in the corner. Old-style camp doors." She had never given any thought to sexual predators or abuse. "I was an extremely innocent child," she says. And, like most gymnasts entangled in training, she says, "Boys were so not on my radar. I'd never had a first kiss. I'd never held a boy's hand, let alone liked a boy."

Nonetheless, she sensed that something was wrong, even though he was the respected Olympic doctor. After the session, she called her mom from the pay phone at the ranch. "It was a lifeline to call home" from the lonely ranch, she says. Her mom was busy at the moment; Jessica could hear her siblings making noise in the background. As a young teen, she wasn't sure how to say what had just happened. She doesn't recall the exact words she used, but she whispered something about thinking she may have been molested. "My mom asked what happened. But I didn't really understand; I didn't know how to say it. I just mumbled, 'I don't know.' My mom said, 'He's the best doctor there is. He's going to help you.' She probably thought I misinterpreted." After all, she notes, if USA Gymnastics backed Larry, how could he be a predator?

Jessica continued seeing him every day that week—until the very last appointment on the final day. "I didn't want to go," she says. "Something felt physically repulsive about it. That was unusual for me; I always did what I was supposed to do." She told her roommates, "I don't want to go to Dr. Nassar." One of the girls sympathized, saying, "Yeah, he touches you funny."

And so, Larry came to the cabin to get her. When he knocked on the door, she was sitting on the floor, her arms around her knees. She huddled tightly up against a bunk bed as he opened the door. "I tensed up. I decided I wasn't going," she says. "I told him I felt sick. He said, 'Are you sure? It's your last appointment.' He was inside the room now. We went back and forth about it. He kept trying to get me to go. But I refused."

She left the ranch and put the unsettling experience with Larry Nassar behind her. "I buried it," she says. She kept pushing herself hard, despite the ongoing hip pain. When she injured her foot during a practice at an Olympic training center in Colorado before a competition, her coach was livid, she says. "She crossed her arms and stared at me, and her face was so tight, she looked like a different person. She told me to get out of her sight." Jessica, unable to participate in the competition with the injury, got banished to her dorm room, with her coach ordering her not to come out until she said so. Jessica stayed in the room for thirty-six hours, leaving only to go to the bathroom. Her mom, who had traveled to the event with her but was not permitted to see her, she says, snuck some food into her room. "Actually, being in the dorm room was a little bit of a relief," she recalls. "I rarely had time to myself." But in the room, she says, "I OCD'ed myself into oblivion," washing her hands repeatedly, running through routines in her mind. Again and again and again. It was her sixteenth birthday.

Jessica has mixed emotions about her parents' role in all of this, noting that while they did tell her she could quit, she wonders, in retrospect, why they didn't just pull her out. "Looking back, I wish they'd stopped me," she says. At seventeen, she was still going, still winning medals, and still mentally spiraling. After the Goodwill Games in 2001, her foot throbbed so badly that she couldn't put her weight on it—and her coach discarded her. "She said she didn't want to keep coaching me. She was furious, like she hated me. It was extremely traumatic; it was like being ripped apart. I still thought she was the key to my success and that she was the reason I got as far as I did. I was a mess at this point. I was not functioning well in any aspect of my life."

Jessica got x-rays on her foot and learned it was broken, meaning she couldn't participate in the next competition, the 2001 world championships. When she found out, she actually felt relieved that she could sit this one out. "It was one of the happiest days of my life," she says. She knew things were out of control. The obsessive-compulsive disorder was still expanding, as it does; now she couldn't take a shower without rubbing her hands repeatedly before washing her hair. In the morning, she had to read an increasing number of news articles before she could start her day. Yet she wasn't ready to let go of the sport. She had been number one in the United States for three years. She still thought she might get to the 2004 Olympics.

But her body had other ideas. She had to have knee surgery, and afterward, she couldn't perform like she had once been able to do. She tried a new coach, then went back to her old coach, who said she hadn't realized Jessica's foot was broken after the Good-will Games, when the coach jettisoned her. The two may not have liked each other, but they needed each other for their careers, Jessica says. They moved forward. In 2003, Jessica was required to compete in a national competition in order to remain a member of the National Team, but she had not yet healed from her injuries. She tried her best amid the injuries and managed to do fine, but it was not a stellar performance like those of her past. It became a defining moment. "I felt like the coaches and judges were done with me. I felt dismissed. I knew then, it's over. To be so easily cast aside, after all that, was devastating," she says. At the same time, she acknowledges, "I did feel free of it."

Once she retired from the sport, it felt strange to enter ordinary life and have free time, and she was not equipped to make the transition. Fortunately, without the stress of training and competitions, her obsessive-compulsive disorder began to ease. But at the same time, her body started changing, causing new anxiety. "I felt like literally overnight, I got a chest," she says. She also got her period; the extreme workouts and low body weight had delayed it. She had a hard time coping with her new body, no longer the perfect sculpture. As a gymnast, she had barely eaten for years and had trained relentlessly every day. But now she was in the normal world. When she saw a reflection of herself in an office window, "I saw that I had a butt," she says. "And I felt obese." If a guy tried to flirt with her, she didn't know how to respond. She had been doing her schooling at home since the fifth grade; she had never really learned how to socialize. She got her high school diploma online and stayed involved with USA Gymnastics, traveling to Europe to help train gymnasts for the world championships. "I didn't want to let the sport go completely out of my life," she says. But her continued involvement was an emotional trigger. In Europe, she was asked to teach ballet to the gymnasts who had replaced her as US Olympic hopefuls, a task she was not mentally ready to do.

One night, alone in a bare dorm room in Bulgaria after the gymnasts had left for the world championships, she cut herself for the first time, with a small pair of sharp nail scissors, on her face. She carved out a deep, round hollow on her forehead, taking her anxiety out on herself. In retrospect, she thinks she may have targeted her face due to the feeling that she was losing her perfect body, her perfect skin, now that she was no longer an elite athlete. "When you're training and not eating much, your skin is perfect," she says. "You look like an angel."

She tried to find a new path and felt more hopeful when she moved to New York City, got a job in a Broadway play, and started attending college. But the trauma from her past still dogged her, and she continued to feel disoriented in her life outside gymnastics. "I had to learn how to eat," she says, recalling how she became highly focused on her weight, trying not to eat any sugar at all. She continued cutting herself, now in places she could cover with clothes, such as her chest. When she cut herself too deeply and frightened herself, she stopped. But it seemed as if every time she got one self-harming behavior under control, another started. Eating became a serious problem, then later, alcohol. She had always thought that once she left gymnastics, she would put it all behind her. She was realizing that it had taken over her life.

In 2009, she had an opportunity to join the board of USA Gymnastics, serving as an "athlete representative." She thought she could use the position to help change the abusive culture of the sport. She would be attending training camps and competitions around the country, connecting with gymnasts. She would be the link between athletes and the board. She imagined herself going to the board meetings and conveying the gymnasts' concerns. She thought about the things she could help change—like the way girls would get so hungry while traveling to competitions, they would hide food from their coaches in obscure places. Maybe she could help fix some of these problems with the sport, she thought, and spare people the kind of emotional pain she suffered.

That's not how it turned out.

"The whole thing was geared toward money and medals," she says of USA Gymnastics. The board meetings were highly structured and efficient; people voted on superficial issues and did not discuss anything controversial, she says. Board members watched uplifting video montages of girls winning medals. They discussed lucrative sponsorships. They went to dinners at nice restaurants on the organization's dime. Once, a sexual abuse case did come up at a board meeting, she recalls, and a lawyer spoke briefly to the group, saying, "We have it covered financially." Then everyone moved on. "They were concerned about lawsuits, not people," she says. The meetings became dangerous emotional triggers: "I would put on a good show at the meeting, then go home and have a breakdown," she says. "I knew I was depressed."

Valorie Kondos Field, the celebrated former coach of the UCLA women's gymnastics team and author of the memoir *Life Is Short, Don't Wait to Dance*, tells me about an incident that highlights the disconnect between officials at USA Gymnastics and the young athletes in its care. Valorie coached many former Olympians and former National Team members on her team at UCLA, and they described the coaching they had endured at the Karolyi Ranch. She says that at the 2012 Olympics in London, she asked Steve Penny, then the president of USA Gymnastics, why the verbally and emotionally abusive coaching was allowed at the ranch. He replied that it produced wins. "He looked at me like I was an idiot," she recalls. Valorie, who grew up in dance, notes that her childhood training was focused not on winning but on performing to the best of her abilities and learning from each performance. It's a style she maintained as the coach at UCLA—to the surprise of the elite gymnasts who joined her team. After years of abusive coaching in their childhood, they were "shocked," she says, when she didn't terrorize them, but rather, encouraged them and got to know them personally.

I sought comment from USA Gymnastics and from an attorney for Steve Penny about these criticisms and did not receive a reply. An attorney for the Karolyis declined to connect me with them.

Meanwhile, Jessica Howard kept trying to find her footing. She began seeing a guy she felt comfortable with, at least at first. Things got serious quickly, until he became possessive and controlling. When he got furious at her for spending time with her sister, she left him. In 2013, she left the board of USA Gymnastics as well. She sought help from a therapist and tried to move forward but remained tangled in depression.

In the fall of 2016, after the *Indianapolis Star* published its exposé on how USA Gymnastics had mishandled reports of abuse against coaches, Olympic medalist Dominique Moceanu called Jessica one night and asked if she had ever been abused. "Dominique is very perceptive," Jessica says. "I was silent for a little while. I remembered the conversation with my mom when I was at the Karolyi Ranch." Jessica had suspected abuse at the time but had "buried it, shoved it down," she says. Things started to click. She told Dominique yes, she had been abused. Jessica thought back to her time with Larry as a young girl. "The memories were very visceral, very real. I could feel the sensations," she says. She thought about the harsh training she had endured throughout her childhood and how it had left her feeling voiceless and vulnerable to Larry. She knew the sport had sparked her battles with self-harm and depression, but she realized it had affected her relationships too, leading her to get involved with the controlling man.

Soon after, Jessica called the *Star*, naming Larry as an abuser—and helping to set in motion his demise.

But Jessica continued to founder, plunging further into depression as she came to grips with how much Larry and USA Gymnastics had taken from her, she says. "I basically didn't leave my apartment. Nothing could get my mind away from the pain. I had no vision for my future. I was sleeping more than people sleep on death row." Alcohol served as a temporary escape, but eventually, she says, "it exaggerated the depression." Sometimes she had thoughts of suicide, although she didn't think she really wanted to kill herself. "I didn't want to die, but I didn't see any purpose in life," she says. She just wanted to find some peace. When her drinking progressed to a perilous stage, she thought maybe it would be best if the alcohol killed her.

The depression eventually grew so deep, it spurred her sister to help her check into a psychiatric ward of a Manhattan hospital. "That was quite sobering," Jessica says. "You are put in a room with another person. They take your clothes, shoes, purse, anything you could use to harm yourself." She recalls the uneasy feeling of being watched—and the fear that if she said something wrong, she could be institutionalized. "It felt like a horror film," she says, recalling the eerie pink walls of her room, the thin mattress, the rose-colored window frame, the room checks at night, and her roommate, a completely silent woman in her eighties. She spent her thirty-fourth birthday in the ward. She manages to joke, "The coffee was inexplicably bad."

After eleven days of intensive therapy and the frightening realization that she could lose her freedom, she says, "I flipped a switch. I thought, I choose my family. I won't leave them." She went home and continued the therapy, meeting regularly with a counselor. She would emerge as an important advocate for children in sports, which we'll see later in her story.

Chapter Fifteen

The Poker Game

A ttorney Jamie White knew the Nassar case would be huge. As soon as he read the allegations in the *Star* in 2016, he started gathering the troops at his law firm in Lansing. He knew that sexual predators don't stop with just one or two victims. He knew something about the minds of predators; he had defended some of them at his practice. And he knew Michigan State, having gone to both college and law school there. He was ready. Soon he and a band of attorneys from around the country would face off in a high-stakes legal battle against his alma mater, brokering a $500 million settlement, the biggest financial settlement of its kind ever in the United States. Getting there would be a game of intriguing, and cutthroat, legal strategy—with a pivotal play by Jamie. As he says, "It was the most expensive game of poker in the history of mankind."

Sitting outside at a Lansing café owned by his wife on a windy, warm afternoon, Jamie is gregarious, down to earth, with an easy smile. But underneath that relaxed vibe lies a fierce litigator. He's getting ready to head across town to a bill signing for legislation he wrote with state lawmakers, allowing more time for child sexual abuse victims to take legal action—crucial for Nassar survivors. Without it, most of the women would not have been able to join civil suits against Michigan State. And the $500 million settlement would not have happened.

Over a club sandwich, Jamie tells me a phenomenal story of the personal journey that led him to the Nassar case.

Jamie learned about crime and injustice from an early age. And he learned the hard way. The biracial son of an African American father and an Irish American mother, he was six years old when he saw his father nearly get killed by a gang of angry men. He grew up in Jackson, Michigan, a small rust belt city once known for manufacturing some twenty brands of cars—and also corsets. "I grew up on the poor side of town," he says. "It was a diverse neighborhood, lots of working poor. I had friends from all different backgrounds." The attack on his father happened on a Saturday afternoon in the summer of 1978. The family had always held backyard barbecues on the weekends, listening to music, playing cards. But this weekend, they planned to do something special. "My parents decided to venture outside the normal comfort zone of our working-class neighborhood and travel to a public lake in southern Michigan," he says. His mom packed a picnic basket, and Jamie was thrilled. "The sun was shining, the beach was full of sand, and the lake was cool. The fact that we were the only family of color at the beach that day was not unusual. It was common that when we traveled outside our neighborhood, we would be the only family of color and almost always the only interracial family."

On the beach, about a dozen guys were hanging out together, drinking heavily—a softball team. The men took an immediate dislike to Jamie's family. "They passed around a bag of baseball bats. Their dogs chased my brother and me into the water, and we weren't swimmers. My dad asked them to leash their dogs, and that went really bad, really fast. My dad got bashed right in front of us. They beat him to within an inch of his life. They cracked his head wide open, with bats and bottles. It was really violent. They were throwing garbage cans and bottles at us. I remember the glass bottles whizzing past me. They chased my brother and me to our car, bashing out our car windows with baseball bats to try to get to us, threatening to kill us," he says. All the while, the men shouted racial slurs. "That was the first real racial experience I had. I was shocked because my parents raised us to believe that we were just the same as everyone else. My grandfather was a civil rights activist, Harold White, a really well-respected man. There's a statue of him in downtown Jackson. It really wasn't until that experience that I saw that kind of hate in people."

During the attack, his father had managed to fend off some of the men, injuring three of them. Those three men got taken to the hospital, along with Jamie's dad. "They actually threw him in the hospital room with those same men," he says. "The guys got off the table and came after him. Then the police came in and read my dad his rights." His father, it seemed, would be the one to get charged. His activist grandfather intervened. "He had some connections. He pressured law enforcement," Jamie says. "Things got turned around, and the three men were charged." The rest of the attackers were never arrested. As for the three who did get charged, justice was not served. Two pleaded guilty to very minor crimes, and the third got acquitted at trial. The defense capitalized on the fact that Jamie's father had injured the men, even though he had done it while fighting for his life against a dozen attackers.

What happened next speaks volumes about Jamie, his family, and the worldview that has shaped his life and his legal work.

"It was an impactful day in my life, for sure. But even more impactful than the crazy violence I saw was the response of my family and my family's friends. They maintained their integrity. They didn't choose to become part of that hate. They just never did that. It would have been easy for them to fold up and blame the world," he says. "Another remarkable thing about that experience was that we had all these deep roots in our community, and when people would come and visit our home as my dad was healing, we had white people coming, black people coming; nobody was a fan of these gentlemen who did that to him, but I never heard anybody change their point of view on how they saw the world. There was a great deal of anger, but there was never hate." To be sure, he says, "That day, that summer, my views of humanity were forever forged, anchored in a deep sense of right and wrong. Instead of focusing on the deeds of the men at the beach, it was the courage of those who came to assist that garnered our attention and gratitude."

Jamie remembers the wise words of his grandfather from the time: "The best way to deal with racism is to buy the company." In other words, get educated, become a success. Jamie took that advice to heart. "It led to my dream to work for myself." He learned a lot from his grandfather, he says, often walking around the neighborhood with him as a young boy, helping him hand out pamphlets, getting minorities involved in civil rights. "I was introduced to the lessons of Dr. Martin Luther King at a very young age. Some of my earliest childhood memories were sitting in on meetings in the living room of my grandfather—he and other local civil rights activists would design action plans associated with improving the political positions of minorities." Jamie worked hard in school and saw his parents work hard too. His mom worked at a local hospital, while his dad made brakes for cars, later becoming a guard and then the warden of a sprawling, walled prison.

His parents had first met at a party when his dad was home from the Vietnam War. The two families get along great now, Jamie says, but that wasn't always the case. His mother's family was wary of his father when the couple first started dating, back in the early seventies. He laughs as he recalls a favorite family tale: when his dad started courting his mom, her brother had a few too many drinks one night and decided it would be a good idea to ride a horse into town to check him out. His dad looked out an open window in the kitchen and saw a horse head staring in at him. "These were the times we lived in," Jamie says. In some states, interracial marriage was still illegal until 1967. The couple married and had three sons.

When Jamie's neighborhood "started deteriorating right under our feet," he says, becoming violent and unstable, the family moved to a safer, "more cookie-cutter" neighborhood, he says. There, he made a new circle of friends and became a football star. In high school, he joined the Army Reserves and waited tables around town to help save for college. He graduated with honors, got a college loan, and headed to Michigan State. "I enjoyed every single minute of it," he says of college. While working toward his degree, he also started working at the Ingham County Prosecutor's Office. He grew interested in law, studying the cases and how the lawyers around him handled them. He went on to law school at Michigan State, while still working in the prosecutor's office. After he graduated and passed the bar exam, he started his own practice—in the attic of a small house he bought in Lansing.

From his attic, he took on all kinds of cases and gradually expanded his firm, later moving to a rented cubicle in a law office. In his first big victory, he won a million-dollar settlement against the City of Lansing when a policeman rammed into pedestrians in his cruiser. He also won a number of high-profile homicide cases. "I never lost a homicide trial," he says. "People would come and watch my closing arguments." Eventually he moved to his own office in Okemos, a suburb of Lansing, and hired a staff, taking on increasingly large and complex cases.

And then came the Nassar case.

"Not to be melodramatic, but honestly, all of that stuff I went through in my life brought me to this," he says. "It started when I was six years old."

His first call in the case came in from gymnast Lindsey Lemke's mom, Christy. Jamie and his wife, Christine, had known the Lemke family for years, and this was personal. Jamie had watched Lindsey grow up in gymnastics. Now a married father of four kids, he felt both heartsick and outraged when he heard Lindsey's story. "I knew this would change that family forever," he says. He was aware of Larry Nassar and his highflying reputation as the Olympic doctor. Jamie's family actually knew Larry's wife, a physician's assistant for a local pediatrician. Jamie's kids had gone to see her for various health issues over the years.

When Jamie studied up on the accused doctor, he says, "I had no doubt that he was going to be the most prolific sex offender in sports history. He had every single tool a sexual predator would want: protection, fame, power. I knew that to have the institutional backing of these major institutions—MSU, USA Gymnastics, the Olympic Committee—would have allowed him to take his grooming to an expert level. I was, unfortunately, confident that there were going to be hundreds of women involved. I remember saying on a local radio show, 'The community needs to brace itself.'"

He was right. But the Lansing community was not quite ready to deal with the predator in its midst. "The community was in denial, in shock," Jamie says. He cites a telling example: as more women came through his door, he tried to book a conference room in downtown Lansing to meet with survivors and attorneys who were taking on clients in the case, including John Manly in California, who represented gymnasts including Rachael Denhollander and Olympic medalist Jamie Dantzscher, the first two women to contact the *Star* and name Larry. The plan was to invite the media and have a press conference about the status of the case. Jamie started calling around to reserve a conference room at the usual places—and got politely declined, time and again. "They didn't want to get involved. No one wanted to be involved with people suing the university," he says. "People were terrified about the university and its coaches coming under scrutiny." These were the early days of the case, he notes, before people understood the full scope of the abuse and the failings at Michigan State that enabled it. The sentiment would change over time, as more facts emerged.

But in the beginning, there was resistance. He finally found a place for the meeting and moved forward.

Far bigger hurdles were yet to come. Jamie knew it would be difficult to make a civil case work. Not only did most of the women fall outside the statute of limitations, but Michigan State had immunity as a government institution. "As a general rule, the state of Michigan and its agencies are immune from civil litigation," Jamie says. "There are some exceptions, but none for sexual abuse." Regardless, he was prepared to give it his all. He hunkered down and got to work. He connected with a Republican state senator, Margaret O'Brien, who was working on a package of sexual abuse laws. They discussed adding two new pieces of legislation to the package—giving survivors more time to take legal action and stripping government institutions of immunity in sexual abuse cases. Jamie got to work, he says, writing the new pieces of legislation behind the scenes.

The legislation was deeply personal for Senator O'Brien. She had known Rachael Denhollander, the first gymnast to report Larry to the *Star*, ever since Rachael was a child. Rachael had helped her knock on doors while campaigning in the early days of her political career, Senator O'Brien tells me. When she learned that Rachael had been abused, it was "a real punch in the gut," she says, and she met with Rachael to discuss what lawmakers could do to protect survivors. "She always had a beautiful smile on her face; she was able to hide her pain from the world," she says, remembering Rachael as a child. "When I thought about it, lots of people in sexual abuse have that mask."

Jamie got to work writing the two new pieces of legislation behind the scenes, he says, recalling, "I started doing twenty-hour days, seven days a week. I hardly saw my family, didn't get to the gym. My diet, health, personal relationships—everything took a back seat. MSU was preparing to dismiss these cases. Other lawyers were telling me I was wasting my time, wasting my money. I felt that there's too much human carnage. There's got to be a solution. There's just no way there can be that much disaster without some remedy."

Jamie says he didn't necessarily need the bills to pass—he just needed to get them to the state legislature for a vote. He believed the pressure of the pending legislation would make Michigan State more willing to make a deal.

His strategy would take a remarkable turn.

Chapter Sixteen

Justice

Women kept coming forward to name Larry as a predator, mostly anonymous at first, meeting with the police, as well as with Jamie White and other attorneys around town and across the country, from Texas to California. The troops were preparing for war—on all sides.

When I meet with a few of the local attorneys in Lansing, including Andrew Abood, Jim Graves, and Mick Grewal, they all tell me how personal the case is to them. They grew up with these girls, with this community. In his redbrick law firm along a highway rimmed with cornfields, Jim tells me, "It was gut wrenching, to hear these stories. You can't help but get emotionally caught up." Hanging in his office is a framed newspaper article about another tragedy that hit the community, the 1988 terrorist bombing of Pan Am Flight 103 over Lockerbie, Scotland. More than a dozen Michigan residents died in the bombing, as the flight's ultimate destination was Detroit. Jim represented one of the families, helping them reach a hard-won settlement.

Across the country in Texas, attorney Michelle Tuegel prepared to join the case as well. As a former top athlete—once ranked first in the United States in women's slalom water skiing—this case was very personal to her too. She says she felt deep empathy with the women who came to her and her partner in the Nassar case, Mo Aziz, for help. And like Jamie White, Michelle knew sex offender cases from all sides. She had worked on a number of high-profile sexual assault cases on the criminal-defense side in the past. "It made me look at the case from the other side," she says. Later she began representing survivors of clergy abuse. Her experience made her a powerful ally for the women in the Nassar case.

At the same time, Larry Nassar assembled his defense team. A local attorney he enlisted, Shannon Smith, tells me something interesting about the beginnings of the case. While she had no idea what the scope of the case would turn out to be, she says, she could see that there would be issues from the start, most notably, a disconnect on Larry's part. "He didn't understand the legal definition of penetration," she says. "He was telling police, 'I don't penetrate.' At the same time, he was showing them videos of himself penetrating. There was a day I sat down with him and said, 'You're penetrating here.' He said, 'That's not penetration.'" When I ask Shannon what Larry thought "penetration" meant, she said, "I can't speak to what he was thinking."

No one can know what is in Larry Nassar's mind, but one thing is clear: he has always maintained his innocence—even after he pleaded guilty. After his plea deal, during the sentencing hearings when all the women gave their statements, he wrote a letter to Judge Aquilina, calling himself a "good doctor, because my treatments worked." The judge read parts of the letter aloud to the court. "It is just a complete nightmare, the stories that are being fabricated to sensationalize this," he wrote. He complained that the attorney general "would only accept my plea if I said what I did was not medical, and was for my own pleasure. They forced me to say that, or they were going to trial and not accepting the plea. I wanted to plead no contest," he wrote, adding that he felt "so manipulated" by the attorney general and judge.

Judge Aquilina's dramatic reading of that last line drew laughter in the courtroom.

"Would you like to withdraw your plea?" Judge Aquilina asked him.

"No, your honor," he said.

"Because you *are* guilty, aren't you?" the judge asked.

No reply. He stood silently.

"Are you guilty, sir?" the judge repeated.

He replied, "I said my plea . . . exactly."

Larry's defense team did not know he was writing the letter to the judge, says his attorney Shannon Smith. "We had no idea."

To be sure, Larry said and did odd things throughout the case, starting with the police interviews in the early days of the investigation. For one, he seemed unprepared to answer a question about whether he became sexually aroused while treating young female patients. When Michigan State Police Detective Lieutenant Andrea Munford asked him that question, he stumbled, first repeating the question and then muttering, "Obviously you don't," according to the police report. The detective informed him that a victim and her mother had seen him with "a visibly erect penis." He replied, "I can't explain that because that shouldn't . . . when I'm working, I'm working, you know what I mean, so I don't . . ."

He also made a point of noting that his young female patients were "usually with their parents" when he treated them. The detective told him he had not worn gloves during the appointment in question and had anally penetrated the victim with his thumb. He said, "If I'm penetrating, it's not penetrating, it's pushing." Then said, "I'm lifting up, it's not going inside her rectum." Then he said that if the condition required him to perform such a treatment, he would use a glove and his index finger.

At one point in the interview, when the detective asked him to explain his technique, he said, "The sacrotuberous ligament runs from the pubic symphysis, the fossa foramen process, it's like the pelvic floor, OK, you wouldn't understand that stuff."

He continued with a baffling discussion of his treatment. "You're coming in towards the labia and go lateral," he said. He gestured with his hands, then said, "So you're going in and apart, and there's muscles that attached to the ligament, so as you're treating it, you can feel the release, and that's a great teaching thing, so I have the students feel the rib cage and then I go and release that, and they're like, oh my god, what did you do, because they can feel that effect." The detective asked what he was feeling when looking for the "release." He said he feels the tissue tension change; then he compared the process to a run in panty hose. He used his arm to show rotation and said it's like wringing out a towel. He said he could go clockwise or counterclockwise. He talked about using "different vector forces" to be effective. He described the process as three dimensional, then demonstrated by tugging on his sleeve. He concluded, "It's that simple."

When asked how long he had been doing the technique, he said, "I have video from thirty pounds ago," then laughed and patted his stomach.

Detective Lieutenant Munford continued pressing him, telling him he had anally penetrated the patient in question with his thumb while vaginally penetrating her with his finger. He stuttered in his reply, saying, "I'm just working the floor. How would I be putting my thumb, and, and, and, and, fingers . . . that would not be correct." The detective said the patient had reported seeing a visible erection during several treatments. He said, "I try my best to be appropriate and professional and . . . I have no understanding of why that would be occurring." The detective kept turning up the pressure. When she asked if he had ever had an erection during treatment, he said, "I'm focused on my treatment. I'm not trying to gain any sexual pleasure out of working with my patients. That's not what being a physician is. That's not what I'm about.

What I'm trying to do is release tissue and work with them, but I'm not trying to get my jollies out of this."

As the detective pressed him further, he continued to stumble. "I'm not purposely trying to get arousal from doing any treatment. I'm not purposely trying to gain some sexual gratification out of doing that. That's not what I'm doing. I mean if there was arousal, it would be because of whatever, I don't know," he said. The detective asked what he meant by the "whatever." He replied, "When you're a guy, sometimes you get an erection." The detective pointed out that men get erections because they're aroused. He replied, "If I had an erection, I don't understand why I would have an erection from doing the treatment; it's embarrassing to have that happen, that's not appropriate, that is just not professional. Yes, you're a guy, but . . . and yes, they're young ladies . . . but I'm trying my best to be professional."

In November 2016, Michigan attorney general Bill Schuette charged the doctor with three counts of criminal sexual conduct, saying this was just the beginning. In December 2016, federal officials indicted the doctor for possessing some thirty-seven thousand images of child pornography, after police found his computer hard drives in his trash.

His wife filed for divorce.

In February 2017, the Michigan attorney general charged the disgraced doctor with twenty-two additional counts of criminal sexual conduct.

Meanwhile, Jamie White and his fellow attorneys around the country tried to reach a settlement with Michigan State, while Jamie worked on the legislation to expand the statute of limitations and strip the university of immunity. "It was a game of chess for months," he says. "I'd come home and tell my wife, 'Oh my god, I'm in checkmate.'"

The bills made it to the state legislature for a vote, putting the heat on Michigan State. Jamie kept tabs on the lawmakers, with the help of a lobbyist, to see which way the wind was blowing for the vote. When it became clear that the bill expanding the statute of limitations would pass, but the bill stripping the university of immunity would *not* pass, he called John Manly and the band of lawyers, who were embroiled in a round of talks with Michigan State in California at the time. Jamie had been at the talks a day earlier but had flown back to Michigan to keep an eye on the impending vote. Michigan State did not know it would keep its immunity, Jamie says. And so he told his team: "Make the deal, now."

They did, to the tune of $500 million.

"The legislative work of the Michigan attorneys and survivors was key to the entire settlement, especially the work of Jamie White, who, along with his team and survivors, worked tirelessly to change the statute of limitations and to attempt to strip the university of immunity," says Michelle Tuegel, the Texas attorney representing the women in the case. "Their efforts continued to build into a massive pressure point as we worked to get Michigan State to settle and compensate our clients. Jamie and his team were the feet on the ground in Michigan who knocked on doors and sat with state legislators. They refused to let legislators forget what happened in Michigan. They insisted that the law needed to change."

She recalls the drama of getting the scoop from Jamie that the university would most likely keep its immunity, putting a potential settlement deal in jeopardy. She was in California at the time, with the band of attorneys engaged in talks with Michigan State. "We all started to sweat as we learned from Jamie that the legislation had evolved from what we had hoped would pass," she says. "Thankfully, Jamie had an inside pulse on what was going down at the Michigan legislature. We learned it was now or possibly never to get a deal inked that would bring at least some peace and healing to our clients."

Noting that "money would not ever repair the damage done to the survivors," she says, "it was the closest we could get for them through our justice system." She adds, "I will never forget the final hours: the sweat, the tears, and the relief were all palpable as the preliminary agreement was signed and passed around the room. Hours and minutes can sometimes mean the difference between $500 million and zero dollars."

Michigan State did not respond to requests for comment on the matter.

In the meantime, prosecutors marched forward with the criminal case, preparing for trial since Larry had not yet pleaded guilty. A few brave young women took the stand and testified against their former doctor in the pretrial hearings, bolstering the case.

Among them, Madison Bonofiglio. She recalls the stress of being asked to identify her abuser in court. "He kind of smirked," she tells me. "It was horrible." Madison had grown up going to Twistars, with the abuse starting around the time she was a preteen. She trusted the doctor, but she did consult with a friend about his disconcerting "treatment." Her friend reassured her, "Oh, he does that to me too." Larry stayed close to Madison on Facebook: "He liked everything I posted," she says, and he zapped her notes on holidays and birthdays, even when she went off to college at Western Michigan University. In college, when she mentioned Larry to gymnasts who hadn't been treated by him, they said his technique sounded weird and wrong. Then Madison read the allegations of abuse in the *Star*. She talked with two of her childhood friends from Twistars, and they decided to go to the police to describe their experience. They were among some of the first to do so following the *Star* report, she says.

She still wasn't entirely sure if what the doctor had done was abuse. "When I first talked to the police, I said, 'I don't know if this is right or not, but this is what happened.' I wasn't sure if I wanted to press charges. I was just telling them what happened. I felt weird about possibly sending a man to jail." She talked with the police a few times, she says, by phone and in person, taking the time out from college to do so. When the child pornography charges came out, she knew for sure that he was an abuser. She moved forward with the police, agreeing to testify against him in the criminal case.

It was "nerve-racking," she says, to be questioned by one of the defense attorneys in court. "He was trying to get me to say the treatment helped me," she says. She adds, "The worst part was that I had to say the words 'vagina' and 'anus' in public." She got through it, but the ordeal of realizing her trusted doctor had abused and betrayed her, followed by the anxiety of testifying against him in court, left some emotional wounds. "It sneaks up on me a lot. If I'm around a bunch of men, it freaks me out," she says, especially if a guy touches her in a crowd, like at a bar. She has a boyfriend of four years who has been very supportive, she notes, adding that she hopes that in speaking out, she will help change the culture of gymnastics.

In July 2017, Larry Nassar pleaded guilty in federal court to child pornography charges. He would later be sentenced to sixty years in federal prison.

In November of that year, he pleaded guilty in two Michigan counties to a total of ten counts of criminal sexual conduct. As part of the plea agreement, he agreed to allow *all* the women who had reported being abused by him through the decades to give victim impact statements at his sentencing hearings, scheduled for early 2018.

But no one expected what was to come in the courtroom.

Chapter Seventeen

The Memory

As the scope of the abuse spread across the press, the survivors had vastly different ways of processing the news. Many did not know they had been abused as children. Some denied it. Others were angry. Some dismissed it. Some knew it was true. Many got mad at themselves. The stories of how each of them came to terms with what happened, reconciling the villain in the news with the friendly man they once trusted, are widely rich, varied, and insightful, as we will see when they unveil their reactions in the coming pages.

Sara Teristi, the gymnast who may have been Larry Nassar's very first target, back in the eighties at Great Lakes Gymnastics, learned of the abuse scandal from her dad. When her father saw the news that Larry had been charged with possessing child pornography, he promptly called his daughter. Sara's first thought: Larry is too smart to get caught for something like that. Busy raising her family in North Carolina at the time, she went on with her life. She did not want to think about those awful years in gymnastics. She had long since buried all of that.

As much as Sara wanted to leave her past behind, however, she could not ignore the widening Nassar scandal in the news. When she saw the women stand up to give their victim impact statements in court, in early 2018, it all came crashing back. As she watched the women tell their stories, she felt a need to hide. "Your first knee-jerk reaction is to protect yourself," she says. "You don't want to see the truth." But she couldn't stop watching. She sat on the floor of her closet, huddled with her cell phone, "hysterically sobbing," she says, as she watched the women on video, confronting Larry, one after another. All of the childhood emotions from her years at the gym came flooding back. "I felt dizzy, like I would vomit," she recalls. She flashed back to John, and Larry, and the way they had treated her, making her feel useless. "It felt like I was having a heart attack." She began to grasp that it was all true. Larry had abused her too. She had tried to talk to the therapist at college and sort through her confusing childhood experience, but she had been dismissed, making her wonder if she was crazy and had made it all up. She had put it away. But now she knew: her instincts had been right.

Her head started whirling; her brain had locked away the memories of her childhood trauma for decades. "My mind was trying to deal with years of suppression and denial," she says. She suffered the first of many panic attacks. She recalls stepping out into the yard and feeling like the sky would fall on her. "I looked up and thought the trees were reaching for me." The memories were coming back, but at the same time, she says, her brain did not want to unearth the full truth of what had happened to her. "I felt like there was a huge, massive object blocking my vision," she says. "I could not see through this black obelisk." She could remember the musty smell from the room at Great Lakes Gymnastics where Larry had abused her. She could remember the physical pain, the feeling of being worthless. She remembered desperately wanting it to stop. But there was something more, still lurking.

It all came back in pieces. When a memory of the anal penetration flashed through her brain, "I collapsed to the kitchen floor. I started screaming and crying so hard, I think I tore my throat," she says. "My husband came home later and said, 'Are you OK?' I looked like hell." She sat down with him, describing the "brain-washing" and abuse of her childhood in gymnastics. He had never known the extent of it. "He was so good, so understanding," she says. Meanwhile, her brain fought with itself. "You go on this teeter-totter as you try to accept the truth. You don't want to accept it. You don't want to go there. You think, No, this didn't happen. Then you think, Yes, it did. You know it did. My brain was arguing with itself, screaming profanities."

She and her husband later talked with their two young sons, who could see that their mom was clearly struggling. "When it's that severe, you can't hide it," she says. "My husband told them, 'Mom is going through something very difficult.' I explained that when I was a child, a doctor did some things he shouldn't have done. He touched me in ways that weren't appropriate." They all talked through it, and the boys were sweet and supportive, she says. Then she talked to her parents. "My dad wanted to know if I blamed them. I said no, not at all. I was the one who wanted to stay in the sport."

In the weeks that followed, Sara continued to feel as if a memory remained lodged in her brain. Part of her didn't want to know what it was. When she and I first met in that serene, misty courtyard at the museum near her home in North Carolina, the memory was pushing its way toward the surface but hadn't made it there yet. She had remembered the potpourri in Larry's bathroom and how the smell of it had given her a dark feeling throughout her life. But she didn't know exactly why.

She and I stayed in touch for months after we met. One day she emailed me and said we should talk. When I called, she told me that the final memory had resurfaced, and it was horrific on a whole new level. She is telling this deeply personal story here for the first time, and it takes courage for her to do so. The memory emerged while she was standing alone in her kitchen, perhaps triggered by a recent doctor appointment, where she had undergone a pelvic ultrasound for a health issue. The sudden force of the recollection left her nauseated and again on her knees on the floor. She remembered being alone in Larry's apartment during the time he claimed to be conducting studies on the girls. She was in her lowest state of emotional distress at the time, having lost all sense of physical boundaries amid the mental abuse from her coach and the physical abuse from her doctor. "He locked the door to his apartment behind us and told me to go to his bedroom," she tells me. "I lay down on his bed, and he started touching my vagina, fingering me. Then he was on top of me, with his mouth down there. He went down on me." Her mind paused as the memory came back. Was that the end of it? She wanted it to be the end. She told herself it surely had to be the end. She got up and left the kitchen, pacing back and forth in the living room. But no. "I knew there was more, but I didn't want to remember. My mind was fighting it," she says. "It was still in self-preservation mode."

The memory forced its way out. "I remembered that he told me to roll over." Her mind paused again, zooming in on that moment when he said to roll over. "And then I saw it," she says. "He anally raped me." She didn't cry. She had been taught to be tough. She had learned to block out physical and emotional pain. She had lost herself completely. "You got very well versed at going to a different place," she says. Afterward, he told her to get up because she had to get back to the gym. Like a robot, she got out of bed and went to the bathroom to clean up. She stuffed some toilet paper in her underwear because she saw blood.

That's when she smelled the potpourri. She finally knew why the scent of it had always haunted her.

The memory solved another mystery too. She had long believed that she left Great Lakes Gymnastics during her senior year because the pain from her injuries had become too great to keep going. But that didn't entirely make sense, because she had joined her high school team after leaving Great Lakes. She clearly wasn't in so much physical pain that she couldn't do gymnastics. With the return of the memory, everything clicked into place: she had left Great Lakes after the rape, never seeing Larry again. On the day she drove to the gym in her Oldsmobile to quit, she had said goodbye to John but had made sure to avoid Larry. Now she understood why.

The return of the memory was "terrifying," she says. "Part of your brain thinks this can't be real. Still, you know it *is* real. It's that brain fight again." But finally, she says, the "black obelisk" that had blocked her view of her past had disappeared. "There was no more questioning what had happened. There wasn't anything else hiding beneath the surface," she says. "There was almost a sense of peace from not fighting this internally anymore. No more trying to piece things together. The puzzle was finally complete."

But there was still a world of healing to do.

Today, she says she wrestles more with the psychological abuse from her coach than the sexual abuse from her doctor. She continues to blame herself for getting injured. It had been so thoroughly drilled into her head that injuries were her fault. She remembers the day she fell from the balance beam, breaking her sternum: there was an instant as she fell through the air when she thought about adjusting her body to possibly land better, but then she figured she would be fine landing in the foam pit. When she landed badly and snapped her sternum, it angered her coach and also led her to the doctor, setting the abuse in motion. She recognizes that she was a child—exhausted, malnourished, and overheated from training in the hot gym with no air conditioning. But still, she says, "I never should have let my body relax. You can never let up."

She is working on rewiring her thinking. It is an ongoing journey. But she is getting stronger, she says, noting, "If I can handle this, there's not a whole lot I can't handle."

Sara has reported the rape to the police. I sought comment about it from Larry Nassar via his attorneys. An attorney replied that the former doctor would not be giving interviews.

Sara had been particularly struck by one of the women who gave her victim impact statement in court, Dr. Danielle Moore, a doctor of clinical and forensic psychology. Danielle, who had gone to Great Lakes Gymnastics in the late eighties and early nineties, like Sara, said in court that despite her success in her education and career, she had struggled throughout her life with feeling worthless, describing it as like being "stuck in a dark room," unable to see through the blackness. She didn't know why she felt this way, she said, until she realized she had been abused as a child. Sara reached out to Danielle since she was a doctor, asking if perhaps she could help her find a therapist near her home in North Carolina, one who would understand the shadowy world of gymnastics and abuse.

The sister army was forming.

Sara eventually found a local therapist—and found a new friend in Danielle.

*****

Danielle Moore speaks with me by phone from Chicago, telling me a phenomenal story. Stunningly, she was serving as a therapist for sex offenders in an Illinois prison when she heard the allegations against Larry. Until then, she did not know that she had been the victim of a sex offender herself. As a child, she had believed Larry was performing a medical treatment.

She had just finished her doctorate at the Illinois School of Professional Psychology and was working on her postdoctorate when her mom called and said Larry had been arrested for sexual abuse. "My immediate thought was, That doesn't surprise me. Then I thought, But *why* doesn't it surprise me?" Driving her car at the time, she pulled over to think about why the news of his abuse had not come as a shock. She thought back to her childhood, to the room at the gym where she saw Larry for treatment. The first time he penetrated her, her dad was with her in the room, and she felt embarrassed. "I remember thinking, I hope my dad doesn't see up my shorts," she says. The penetration continued, and it was so uncomfortable, she came up with a plan. "I started wearing tighter shorts, hoping he couldn't get in." In her tight shorts, she says, "I tried to shrink into myself. I tried to make my vagina closer to my stomach, to keep him away." At the same time, Larry pretended to be her friend, using his favorite tactics of bringing her little gifts from the Olympics and connecting with her on Facebook. When Larry's wife had a baby, Danielle and her mom went out shopping and bought a baby book for his child.

"My mind was spinning," Danielle says, as the truth came into view. She had been abused. Larry's treatment was not medical but sexual. As an expert in psychology, she says, "I could see the grooming, the gifts, the manipulation. I thought, Why didn't I know it? But I was a kid; I didn't have a doctorate degree back then." She adds, "I had kept Larry high on a pedestal. He was a doctor, a friend; he manipulated and groomed, and there was the power dynamic. There's no seeing through that as a kid." She thought about all the girls Larry had access to at the gym. Having counseled serial sex predators, she knew he must have taken full advantage of that access. She told her mom, "This is going to be huge."

She came to realize that the sexual abuse of her childhood helped explain many things in her life, including an abusive marriage she had entered into at age nineteen. After getting divorced, she had thrown herself into her education, racking up two master's degrees and the doctorate. "I was trying to make myself feel more worthy," she says. She was also coping with surgery after surgery to her back and spine from old gymnastics injuries, while battling health insurers over enormous bills. Amid all of this, she had no time to think about her past—and no desire to do so either.

Interestingly, she says, she actually felt safe in the prison while counseling the sex offenders. They were narcissistic, manipulative, dangerous predators, she says, but they were out in the open. "I knew who they were. They weren't hiding anymore. Often when you walk into a place, you don't know who's good or bad. In that prison, I knew," she says. "And I was the one with the power and authority." She resigned from the job once she realized she had been targeted by a sex offender, because it was a conflict of interest, and she sought help at a trauma treatment center. She continues to do therapy for depression and anxiety, she says, noting that the bills for the treatment cause more anxiety—an issue many survivors have to cope with as they await payments from the Michigan State settlement. She tries to avoid emotional triggers, such as news stories about the Nassar scandal or stories of women who get dismissed or disbelieved when they report abuse. When Dr. Christine Blasey Ford accused Supreme Court nominee Brett Kavanaugh of teenage sexual assault, "I went through a huge funk," she says. "I know other survivors did too."

She appreciated having the chance to confront Larry in court, even though she knew it would be extremely unnerving to face him and give her statement. "You're facing your worst fear head-on," she says. "I practiced beforehand, talking to a picture of him to desensitize myself." Standing in court, looking composed, with a pierced eyebrow and her straight blond hair falling on her shoulders, she fixed her blue eyes on Larry and said, "I want you to be remorseful, apologetic, and truly understand all the pain that you have caused and still cause. However, I don't believe that you are capable of this kind of empathy. But I am sure that you do feel sorry for yourself. So I hope that your self-pity is as dark and more terrifying than my feeling of worthlessness."

Standing before him "felt strange, like the courtroom was getting smaller," she says. But she said what she needed to say—and her words packed a punch: "Mr. Nassar, you are no longer called a doctor. You have been stripped of your medical license, and soon you will be known by your prison number for what I hope to be the maximum sentence. I find this fitting, as I was a thing, inhuman, or just a number to you. While your name and former title fade, I hope being reduced to a number will define you, as it has defined me for so many years. However, I pride myself on characteristics that you do not possess: caring, empathetic, and continually earning the respect of my patients, which is why I will no longer be known as a number—and I will be known as *Doctor* Danielle Moore."

———

Chapter Eighteen

Freedom

For Shelby Root, the gymnast who says she was groomed into a sexual relationship with John Geddert when she was an isolated eighteen-year-old, the Nassar scandal ended up freeing her—from her own mind. She had never been able to stop blaming herself for her painful experience with her former coach, who had eventually discarded her, she says, leaving her depressed to the point of feeling suicidal. "I always looked back and thought, I should've known better. The devastation affected me, and my relationships, throughout my life. I had serious trust issues for decades."

Shelby had attended Great Lake Gymnastics before Larry arrived, and she never knew him. But now, learning what he had done, and thinking back to the culture of the sport she had grown up with, she began to feel that she had been carefully groomed by John, she tells me, and that she was not to blame. She could see that she had been used, she says, and that he should not have initiated sex with a vulnerable teen he had trained at his gym. "He had no boundaries," she tells me, adding, "but he forgot that we would all grow up." She called Dr. Seann Willson, the friend she had known since childhood, and said, "I don't think this was my fault." Seann replied, "I've been waiting thirty years for you to say that."

Shelby moved forward in a relationship with a man she had been seeing and got engaged to be married, finally able to trust herself, and him.

In August 2017, nearly a year after the Nassar scandal first hit the news, Shelby received a jarring string of messages from John Geddert through Facebook. She sends me the exchange. It began:

Hey Shelby, can you give me a call when you get a chance . . .

She did not reply. Then, a couple of hours later, another note from him:

Fairly important.

Again, no reply from her. Later he tried to call her through Facebook. Then he sent another note:

Whooops that was a pocket dial . . . didn't even know you could call a Facebook address.

Once again, she did not reply. A couple of hours later, he tried to call through Facebook again. Wanting to shut it down now, she replied, saying:

Hi John, I have to say your message caught me off guard as we haven't talked in over 25 years. I am in a very good place in my life right now. I am very happy and recently got engaged to the most amazing man I have ever known. I'm certain he is better than I deserve, but he truly and completely loves me and I him. So I will decline to contact you and respectfully ask that you do the same. I would like to leave the door to this part of my past closed and focus on what lies ahead.

And he replied:

> I am very happy for you and I would not contact you if it
> were not important . . . there seems to be some investi-
> gation going on concerning our past . . . I am sure those
> behind it only want to do me harm . . . If you want to know
> what I know I would be glad to share. Honestly I meant you
> no disrespect.

Shelby already knew that he was being investigated. She had
been contacted months earlier by an official at the watchdog US
Center for SafeSport. The group had suspended John after the
Nassar scandal and started an investigation amid complaints about
his coaching. During the investigation, SafeSport had learned of
his inappropriate behavior with Shelby, she says. She exchanged
emails with an investigator, which she shared with me, and she
also talked with him by phone. He was "very sensitive," she says,
helping her think through the entire experience and see it from a
broader perspective. It was another step, she says, in accepting that
she was not to blame for the manipulations of her former coach.

An official at SafeSport told me the group does not comment
on specific investigations.

In January 2018, Shelby watched the stream of women stand
up and confront Larry Nassar in court. "I heard the judge say,
'You're not victims. You're survivors.' It was the most empowering
thing I'd ever heard. I didn't want to be a victim. I didn't want to be
weak," she says. "It took me thirty years to figure that out."

In August of that year, Shelby got married, in a beach wedding
in Fiji. She sends me photos of the couple standing on the sand,
beaming at each other, with her in a white gown and him in a pale
gray suit, the teal waters of the ocean stretching into the distance.
They live in Australia now. They had met and dated seriously years
earlier, back when she was having a hard time trusting men. He

had wanted to move the relationship to the next level and share a future, but she didn't think she could do it. She was still wrestling with the ghost from her past. A couple of years ago, he emailed her out of the blue, and they reconnected, falling in love again; this time, she was ready. She had made peace with herself.

Shelby told him about her history with her former coach, and he listened and empathized. She talked with her mother as well, telling her, "You know, you were part of the grooming process too." John had endeared himself to her mother, securing her trust. Her mom hadn't known the signs of grooming. "Neither of us did. But now we do," Shelby says. "My mom wrote me a letter, apologizing, telling me, 'I don't know why I didn't intervene. You needed me and I wasn't there.'"

Shelby and her mother, who are now close, hope that by going public with this story, they will help other girls and their parents understand the grooming process—and spare them the lifetime of pain that it can cause. It takes guts for Shelby to share her story publicly here for the first time, providing key insight into the saga of the coach and doctor who climbed to Olympic heights, leaving a trail of damaged girls.

While Shelby closed the door to her past, many women were about to open that door, with no idea what lurked on the other side.

Chapter Nineteen

Facing the Truth

Lindsey Lemke, the Twistars gymnast who met with me in the early months of the Nassar scandal, didn't believe the allegations of abuse against her old friend Larry when they first came to light. She thought he had performed a legitimate medical treatment, as he had always claimed.

She was starting her junior year at Michigan State in the fall of 2016 when she heard the news. She and her friends on the school's gymnastics team suddenly got called into an urgent meeting. The head coach, Kathie Klages, and others from the athletic department gathered together with the gymnasts, she recalls. The way Lindsey remembers it, the coach said, "We have some really, really shitty news to tell you guys. Well, in my opinion it's really shitty." Allegations against Larry were about to hit the news, the coach said, without giving any details.

"They didn't tell us what kind of allegations," Lindsey says. "All they basically told us was that we weren't allowed to say anything to anybody about it, including our families. They said if anybody calls you about it or any media sources ask, don't say anything to them about the situation. Essentially we left that meeting feeling like OK, we're literally not allowed to tell anybody about it."

"So the first thing Lindsay does, she gets out her phone and calls me," says her mother, Christy. She started googling. The news soon appeared online, when the *Indianapolis Star* published the allegations of sexual abuse.

Lindsey couldn't believe Larry would hurt anyone. Neither could her teammates at Michigan State, she says, at least not at first. Her mother, however, was concerned. She asked Lindsey if Larry had abused her, and Lindsey said no. "I thought what he did to me was a legit treatment, not sexual abuse," Lindsey explains. As the news spread across the media, Lindsey ignored it—the news made her angry. "I felt like, you people are awful. How do you try to ruin this guy's life that literally did everything for you?" She kept focusing on gymnastics, while her mom kept asking if she had been abused. Christy had an increasingly bad feeling. She and Lindsey were close and had always talked about everything, but Lindsey kept saying no, she had not been abused. "Every time she'd ask me, I'd get mad," Lindsey says. "I'd be like, 'Stop asking me.'" Lindsey continued to believe that the doctor's treatment was medical. He was her trusted mentor and confidant. She could not see him as an evildoer.

In December 2016, amid Lindsey's repeated and adamant denials, her mother had a moment when she thought that perhaps the allegations were indeed questionable. She texted her long-time friend Larry and said, "We're thinking of you." When she didn't hear back like she usually did, she wondered what was up. She checked the news to see if there were any new developments. That's when she saw the arrest for child pornography. "I was disgusted," she says. "My stomach sank."

She and Lindsey's father broke the news to Lindsey, and that's when the horrendous truth came into focus. "I realized, OK, what he did to me was not right," Lindsey says. "I was like, OK, I need to rethink what actually happened. It was sexual abuse." In that moment, she says, "I just remember feeling betrayed. Obviously he's messed up mentally. I mean, no person who's right in their mind does that." But that's no excuse, she adds, because he knew that it was wrong. It was "mind blowing," she says, to make the transition from defending Larry to recognizing him as a predator. "That's the best way I know how to put it."

She began looking back through her childhood and "connected all the dots," figuring out how it happened. "I was like, he took me into his basement because he didn't want his wife and kids to be around. He would have me go over to his house because that's the most private spot to do it. He never billed our insurance because then there's no evidence that it was happening. He gave me gifts to gain my trust. He became friends with my parents to gain their trust. So many things came together."

An outraged Christy called coach Kathie Klages to discuss the situation. The coach defended Larry, insisting that he had performed a medical procedure, Christy says. The coach also suggested that the child pornography could have been planted, she says. Lindsey and her mother were furious at the coach for trying to protect Larry. Lindsey, meanwhile, had to keep working with the coach at Michigan State, which was "just the hardest thing," she says. "I still had to go in the gym every day and listen to her. It was unbelievable. This was my head coach, who was supposed to be looking out for me." One day, Lindsey says, the coach asked the team if they wanted to sign a card for Larry.

I asked attorneys for Kathie Klages if she would like to comment on the allegations cited in this book. An attorney responded that she is innocent of the charges against her.

Lindsey became one of the first courageous women to publicly identify herself as a Nassar survivor, speaking out about her experience in the early months of the scandal in 2017, a time when many survivors remained anonymous.

Nearly a year later, with her brother standing by her side in court, she blasted both Larry Nassar and John Geddert in her victim impact statement. But first, she praised the women who had taken the stand before her. "I first want to start out by saying how proud I am of every single person in this room and everywhere that have used their voice to speak their stories," she said. "You are all an inspiration to me, and without all of you, I wouldn't be standing up here speaking right now."

Then she destroyed Larry. "Today I am speaking to you as my ten-year-old self, on behalf of her. So I hope that is who you picture standing up here looking at you right now. I have my arm wrapped around her," she said. "Today I get to see what my life will be like without you for the first time in twelve years. Today I will finally be free. Larry, to me, you are the worst type of person, someone who takes advantage, someone who belittles, someone who controls, someone who took away trust, childhoods, happiness, innocence, and someone who even took lives of others." However, she said, she has prevailed: "Today I speak to you because us women, we are stronger than you thought we ever were. We control you. We together will rise while you fall."

And then she took on John. "Since you are too much of a coward to be here in court today and this week, I hope you are watching and listening to me right now. You and Larry carry a lot of the same characteristics," she said. "You are a disgrace. You coached us, your athletes—who paid you thousands and thousands of dollars—by fear, to control us and to purposely scare us. Well, John, you are now the one who has failed, not us," she said. "My teammates and I spent way too many days as innocent children shaking, crying, trembling, some even trying to take their own lives, because of you. You brainwashed me, and so did Larry. I couldn't speak up for myself because I was seen as disrespectful; I didn't have a voice, but now I do. So I hope you are ready. You, John Geddert, also deserve to sit behind bars, right next to Larry."

A couple of days earlier, Lindsey had asked her mother to read a statement on her behalf, which her mom had done. But when Lindsey saw all the women standing up, she felt inspired to join

THE GIRLS | 187

them. She asked prosecutor Angela Povilaitis for the green light to read a statement and got it. Judge Aquilina approved, telling Lindsey in court, "I appreciate you wanting to also come forward personally." Later, after her blistering statement, John Geddert tried to quiet her, she says. He contacted a mutual friend and said to tell Lindsey to stop talking about him, she tells me. Lindsey did the opposite. She tweeted about him. She says, "It's almost comical, the fact that he still thought he could intimidate me."

I spoke with both Lindsey and her mom in the months following their court statements in 2018, and the difference between the first time I met them and this time was profound. When we first met, in the early months of the scandal in 2017, they seemed sort of shell-shocked by the duplicity of their friend Larry. No more. Now they are on fire—a vocal force for change. Lindsey regularly excoriates enablers of the abuse across the media. During Larry's sentencing hearings, she happened to see Lou Anna K. Simon, then the president of Michigan State, talking to reporters, and Lindsey took the opportunity to publicly confront her, demanding accountability. Later, Lindsey created a very moving "Survivor Series" on YouTube, describing her personal experience and empowering others.

But it hasn't been easy finishing her degree at Michigan State. As the scandal widened, exposing tremendous failings at the university, her coaches on the gymnastics team never discussed it, she says, which she found disappointing. She retired from the team when she got injured, at the advice of a doctor and trainer at the university, but then wondered if she should have trusted them since they were friends with Larry—an understandable concern.

Michigan State vastly failed the girls and the Lansing community in allowing the abuse to continue for decades—and then shirking responsibility when the truth got exposed. When the Michigan attorney general launched his investigation of the school after the Nassar sentencing in 2018, investigators found that the university failed in many ways, including "issuing misleading public statements, drowning investigators in irrelevant documents, waging needless battles over pertinent documents, and asserting attorney-client privilege even when it did not apply." The actions "highlight a common thread," the investigation found: "MSU has fostered a culture of indifference toward sexual assault, motivated by its desire to protect its reputation."

Lindsey says she strives to stay strong and be "the bigger person," getting her degree and helping survivors understand: "Your voice matters."

*****

Lindsey's friends Presley Allison and Taylor Stevens—the two best friends who left Twistars for their high school team—are emerging as important voices for women as well.

When they learned of the allegations against Larry, they realized, with horror, that he had abused them too. Taylor remembered how her younger self had suspected him of abuse, and she had asked Presley and other friends what they thought. When they said he performed the same procedure on everyone, Taylor figured it must be legitimate since he hadn't singled her out. It pained her to realize that she hadn't trusted her gut. She had to remind herself that she was a kid at the time.

Taylor and Presley tell me about the difficult conversations they had with their parents when the news broke. Taylor called her mom late one night from college as soon as she read the *Star* report. "I said, 'Mom, did you see this?' She said, 'Did this happen to you?' I said yes. We both started crying. She didn't understand at first why I hadn't told her. That was hard. I felt like she thought I didn't trust her. Eventually she understood, but it took a while for our relationship to get back to where it was. I felt bad that I hadn't told her, but I was a kid."

Presley had an emotional conversation with her mom as well. When her mother asked if Presley had seen the shocking news,

Presley said, "Mom, you were there." Her mother had been in the room during the abuse, but the doctor had strategically obstructed her view, as usual. "I always thought she knew," Presley says. "She was devastated. She felt really guilty. I think she still does. She was like, 'When did it happen? How did I miss it? What else did I miss?'" It took some time for Presley to talk with her father about it. "That's not a conversation you ever want to have with your dad," she says. Taylor agrees. She also needed some time before she talked with her dad. When she did, she says, "He started crying. It was rough. My parents both apologized. It was hard to hear them say they're sorry. I told them it was not their fault. I felt like I should be apologizing for not telling them. It forever changes your relationships."

With the scandal in the news every day, Presley says, her college professors discussed it in class, making it difficult for her to attend. Meanwhile, Taylor went to file a report with the police. "I wanted to make sure it was known to Michigan State that he had done this," she says. She had to talk to a young male officer, and the interview was uncomfortable. "At that point, no one really knew all the details of what Larry had done; I had to answer all these awkward questions and to see his facial expressions. It was awful. I kind of shut down after that." She was in nursing school, and, like Presley, she heard people discussing the news nonstop. At the same time, she says, the experience made her feel all the more passionate about going into the medical profession. She tells me, "I want to be that person advocating for patients."

Presley and Taylor both had stinging words for Larry in their court statements, which were read to the court by advocates. Presley described how she had worried about writing a statement because she hadn't been abused as many times as other people. Then she realized, "Whether it was one time or one hundred times, once is one time too many." Taylor hurled this fireball: "You have stripped me of my innocence, my dignity, and my youth, but you will not take away my rights as a woman to stand up to predators like you."

Chapter Twenty

The Family

zzy Hutchins, the gymnast who had trained and competed with a broken leg, defended Larry when the news of the scandal broke. Her family tried to help her get to the truth, but she believed in him, trusting that his treatment had been medical. "Larry was one of the best people I knew, or at least I thought I did," she says. "He was my friend." As the weeks passed and she continued to stand by him, her boyfriend, Cody Igo, tried a new approach: he called on her old friend Lindsey Lemke.

Lindsey was becoming a leader in the emerging army of survivors.

She and Izzy had been friends since their childhood days at Twistars. When Cody texted Lindsey for help, she was on it. She understood, having gone through her own phase of disbelief that Larry had abused her while pretending to treat her. She promptly texted back:

> I think the best thing you can do for her is to just reassure her that she did nothing wrong, and there was no reason for her to know what was going on. This doesn't define who she is, and she is still capable of amazing things, regardless of what he makes her feel like through this. Izzy is seriously

one of the most kick-ass people I know, and she has SO much to offer with such a big heart, no one, not even him, can take that away from her.

Cody texted in reply:

You're such an amazing person and for that I thank you. People put strong girls like you in this world to fight for others!

With the help of Cody, Lindsey, and her family, Izzy came to understand that Larry had indeed betrayed her. The realization hit her "like a truck," she says. "I had to go back through all these memories and change them. All those things Larry did for me, all those gifts he gave me, our friendship, it was all a lie. It was all a part of his manipulation so that I would trust him and he would be able to do his sick treatments on me." As she tried to wrap her head around his deceit, the stress and sadness led her to look for an escape in cutting herself, as she had done while at Twistars. Cody noticed immediately and helped her stop. Then came the nightmares, transporting her back to the massage table beside the fireplace in Larry's basement. "It felt so real, like I could feel the heat of the fireplace, and I could feel his hands on me again," she says. She would wake up in a panic, sobbing and gasping for breath.

Her sister, Ireland, attempted to come to grips with the realization that she had been abused as well. The family was in emotional chaos. It pains me when Izzy's mother, Lisa, tells me that she blames herself, when the blame is on the predator who so cunningly manipulated her family. Lisa lies awake in bed at night, she says, her mind racing with thoughts of her daughters and the abuse they endured. "I let them down. I didn't protect them. I allowed this to happen. I'm angry. I'm hurt. I feel betrayed, not only by Larry, but by MSU, Twistars, John, and USAG," she says. "It breaks my heart to see my daughters' father break down and cry. Watching his eyes close, his chin and shoulders lower and fall forward, as he has to listen to what Larry did. What father ever wants to hear that?" She wonders now, "Will my girls ever be safe?"

Izzy's father, Eric, began suffering seizures from stress when he learned the hideous truth. He had considered both Larry and John to be friends: "Look what they built over the years—the Olympic head coach and his sidekick. At all costs. Look at how many lives were ruined. It's sickening, extremely sickening." Like Lisa, he tortured himself over the fact that he had trusted the doctor. He thought about all those seemingly thoughtful texts Larry had sent, expressing concern about Izzy's injuries. Eric had believed that the doctor truly cared for his children. He thought about how Larry had come between him and Lisa, playing them against each other with his lies, contributing to the couple's eventual split.

Fortunately, Eric has found comfort in family and friends, who are "very supportive," he says. "They don't understand how it happened. I don't understand how it happened either. But across the board, they have been sympathetic." He tries to keep the anxiety under control, noting, "As a family, we'll get through it. The kids have their health. They're in school; they're getting educated. And there's a powerful movement out there—a powerful movement for change." He hopes his story will be a part of that change, helping to spare other families from such a fate.

Indeed, that hope is what motivated the entire family to speak with me, despite the pain of revisiting the past—and the vulnerability of putting themselves in the public eye. They want people to understand how predators groom and manipulate the parents as well as the kids, and the staggering effects of the abuse across the family. Izzy had encouraged her parents to talk to me after she met with me in Lansing, Cody by her side, at the Italian restaurant where she told me her unthinkable story. Later, Ireland decided to publicly identify herself as a survivor for the first time in this book as well. The two sisters are courageous young voices.

There is still much healing to do.

Izzy continues to suffer from emotional triggers, such as making a doctor appointment or seeing a massage table. She does not go to doctors alone anymore. Sometimes she struggles with intimacy, flashing back to what Larry did. She wonders if she will have physical pain for years to come from the injuries that Larry failed to properly treat—and if things would have been different if she had received legitimate care. She worries about the mounting bills for therapy.

With the help of Cody, her family, and friends, Izzy is striving to move forward, and she is helping her younger sister do the same. When Izzy confronted Larry in court, Ireland and Cody stood beside her like a pair of sentinels. Ireland wasn't ready yet to publicly identify herself as a survivor, but she says she felt proud and inspired watching her older sister take the stand. Izzy, meanwhile, feeling nervous as she began her statement, started speaking fast. Judge Aquilina asked her to slow down, saying, "Wait a minute. We're not racing. You have as much time as you need." Izzy smiled. Then she took a breath and told her wrenching story—with a cardboard box full of gifts from Larry serving as visual aids.

In a heartbreaking scene, she held up the childhood gifts, one by one, starting with a figurine of the mascot from the 1996 Olympics—the cartoony character called Izzy. Then she held up a little metal box of bandages, saying, "There were Izzy Band-Aids for Izzy boo-boos, because of all the injuries I had." Next she displayed a greeting card Larry had sent along with the gifts. She read his words aloud: "Dear Izzy, I am so proud of you having such an awesome season this year. Did you know that the 1996 Olympic mascot was Izzy? Well, enjoy. And, of course, I have a pair of Izzy socks from the 2000 Aussie Olympics. Love you, girl. Larry."

She described the abusive environment of Twistars and how she had harmed herself amid the pressure and stress—and she had some choice words for coach John Geddert. "John, I find it funny that you tried to keep us all silent for so long, and now you're the one who is silent. We found our voice and we are calling you out, but you are nowhere to be found, hiding and hoping that you can just sneak out of this, but you can't. And we will come for you next."

She closed by facing Larry head-on, her dark eyes flashing. She said she had grown up wanting to be a doctor, just like him, and had begun studying medicine in college. When she realized he was a sexual predator, she said, "I was so sickened that I couldn't stand the thought of being anything like you. I wanted to throw all I had done away." Then, a breakthrough. "I realized something: You were never a *real* doctor. You did not heal me; you only hurt me. And I hope that eventually, I can bring good back into the medical community. I promised myself I would continue and go to medical school and become the doctor that you never were."

Judge Aquilina praised her strength, saying, "You have a voice, and your words are so important, and I hope now you begin the real healing, because you matter. Do not self-harm. Do not do any of those negative things. You are a positive role model—survivor. Please continue on this path and with that lovely voice of yours."

When Izzy left the stand, she noticed a garbage can—and dumped Larry's gifts in the trash.

Chapter Twenty-One

The Teen Warriors

For sixteen-year-old Autumn Blaney, the Olympic hopeful who got fed up and left the sport at thirteen, Larry's betrayal caused painful issues of trust with the men she loved the most—her father, her older brother, and her grandfather. Suddenly she was afraid to hug them, or to be alone with them. "I had such guilt about it," she says, recalling how she froze when her grandfather touched her on the shoulder at church. "But I felt like I couldn't trust anyone anymore." After all, Larry had been like a family member, and look what he had done.

It had taken some time for Autumn to believe that Larry was a sexual predator, not a doctor who had given her medical treatment. "It was so confusing because he did so much for everyone. I always thought of bad guys to be like John. John was the bad guy. I never, ever thought it would be someone like Larry," she says, adding, "That's how he got away with it for so long." Her mom, Kris, found it hard to believe the worst as well. When Larry got arrested for child pornography, they could both see the truth. "Finally, I understood," Autumn says. "I thought about everything that had happened, and I understood."

Kris remembers seeing the arrest on the news, feeling gutted. "I just felt such guilt that this happened under my nose," she says.

"I felt I had failed at my most important job." I remind her that the abuse is on the abuser. Kris had always kept a very watchful eye over Autumn, accompanying her to practices at the gym and on all her travels to competitions. Larry was a master by the time he met the family, after decades of sharpening his skills.

Autumn fell into depression. "I isolated myself. I was constantly thinking, I'm a victim, I was sexually abused. I'd hyperventilate. I couldn't feel my arms or legs. I'd sit there and just not stop crying. It's awful, to have to live with it. I felt confused, angry. I was so consumed with it. I felt like a complete crazy person all the time." When she spent the night at a friend's house for a birthday party, a nightmare invaded her sleep. "I had a dream that he was abusing me and I realized it was abuse," she says. "I told myself not to cry." Sometimes she had panic attacks and blamed herself for having them. "I was so trained to blame everything on myself. I was so mad at myself. My emotions were everywhere."

She didn't want anyone to know she had been abused. "I was like, I just want to wear a bag; I don't want anyone to look at me. I just felt nauseous if someone were to look at me. It wasn't so much when my age group looked at me—I felt like I could protect myself with them—but with adults, like Larry's age, I was constantly aware," she says. "Because I was trained to hide emotion, that made it even harder. I had to train myself, to tell myself it's OK to go through this." She began staying up late at night, obsessively googling news on the scandal. "I would be crying. I would pray, please let me control my thoughts."

Kris struggled with online trolls. "I finally had to cut myself off of Facebook. I saw all these posts, saying, "How did parents let this happen? What's wrong with these parents? I would never let this happen to my kids." She sighs and says, "I'm the most protective parent in the universe." Autumn nods and agrees, saying, "I just wanted to comment on every one: This can happen to anyone. Don't be so high and mighty. It can happen to you."

And then one day, Autumn turned a corner. "After a few months of depression, I decided, I'm not controlled by someone." She posted a brief statement on Facebook, publicly identifying herself as a survivor: "My name is Autumn Blaney and I am no longer going to hide. This is very hard for me to say, but I feel that this is going to help my healing process. I am one of the many survivors that has been sexually abused by Larry Nassar," she said, describing her anxiety as she realized that her trusted doctor had abused her while pretending to treat her. "I am strong and I will get through this struggle. I know now that what Larry did to me was NOT my fault. I am still continuing through my pain, but I am a fighter and I am going to get through this."

As she posted the statement, she says, "I remember sweating, shaking, being afraid of people judging me. Then I got all this support, and I was like, OK, this was definitely the right thing to do. I got a lot of comments from the sister survivors. Jordyn Wieber sent me a bracelet that said, 'Together We Rise.'"

In the spring of 2018, Autumn bravely spoke at a press conference in Texas, with her mom by her side. Autumn and other survivors, including Olympic medalist Jamie Dantzscher, called on Texas officials to more aggressively investigate crimes at the Karolyi Ranch, the National Team training center where Larry got his hands on top gymnasts. "Jamie held my hand when I was speaking. I didn't have anything prepared. I was holding her hand so tight, I felt like I was going to fall on the ground," Autumn says. "My legs were shaking." Afterward, with the weight of her secret lifted, and with the newfound strength in her voice, she realized she could use her experience to help other girls and fight for change.

She focused on healing, and on getting back to her life that Larry had pushed off track. She became very interested in a new, more serene sport—golf—and quickly excelled. She also found a calming outlet in making schedules for golf events and other aspects of her life. "I make a schedule now for like two weeks," she says. "It helps me feel in control."

"She loves schedules," her mom says, and the two exchange glances and laugh.

"I like crossing things off lists," Autumn says.

Her mom teases her about how her schedules include appointments for hanging out with friends. "Yup, that's in the schedule," Autumn says with a grin.

As Autumn moves forward with her life, she says, "I'm happy that I'm not brainwashed anymore." She pauses for a moment and thinks big picture: "There's no step-by-step guide for how to deal with this. I had always been told exactly what to do my whole life—what to do to become an elite. With abuse, everyone deals with it differently. It's a very interesting process." She is starting to feel more comfortable around the men in her family. She recently gave her grandfather "a little side hug," she says, which made him happy. "He was like, 'That meant a lot to me.'" She says she might write her own book one day, and I hope she does. She is one wise sixteen-year-old.

A few months after we met in Lansing on that early Sunday morning, I learned that Autumn had signed with Cleary University in Michigan to compete on the women's golf team. She plans to get her degree in sports management—putting those scheduling skills to use. Her new coach, Bob Fillipps, said in the announcement of the news, "I'm very excited about signing such an outstanding player in Autumn." He got that right.

*****

For fifteen-year-old Emma Ann Miller, the dancer who is most likely the very last survivor in the decades-long travesty, the allegations of abuse in the news didn't immediately click—but it didn't take long until they did. Once she started hearing the stories of other women, she told her mom, "I believe them. I believe them all." Their stories were much like hers, and she realized that Larry's "treatment" was not medical. Emma Ann has since become a mighty advocate for women and girls. When Michigan State closed a fund to help survivors pay for therapy, she stood up and spoke passionately to the university's board of trustees—and helped get that fund reinstated.

Standing up in court, with her mom, Leslie, by her side, Emma Ann gave a statement that was both poignant and burning hot. While she was a picture of grace and composure, she had fire in her eyes and in her words. "Your Honor, it's always been just my mom and I. I needed a positive male role model in my life. Nassar filled that spot for me. He has known me since my mom gave birth to me and has watched me grow up. I trusted him like a family member. There has never been a time in my life when I didn't know Larry Nassar. But now I wish I never met him," she said. "He put my picture up on his wall with the Olympians. I thought I mattered to Larry. I thought I was special."

Looking straight at Larry, she said, "I have never wanted to hate someone in my life, but my hate towards you is uncontrollable. Larry Nassar, I *hate* you." As she said the words, her anguish was palpable. Then she gathered herself and continued with the poise of someone far beyond her years: "I will work on forgiving you, as I know that is what God wants, but at this moment, I will leave forgiveness up to him." Emma Ann asked the judge for the maximum sentence, noting that in federal prison, Larry will have access to "actual medical treatment," unlike the girls in his care. Then she told her abuser, "But don't get too excited, Larry. You'll probably never talk to a woman again, except for one holding a gun, a taser, and a billy club."

As for Michigan State, she had these fiery words: "Now to MSU. Are you listening, MSU? I can't hear you. Are you listening? My name is Emma Ann Miller and I'm fifteen years old and I'm not afraid of you, nor will I ever be. At fifteen, I shouldn't know the inside of a courtroom, but I'm going to become real comfortable in one. So should you."

She had something to say to the world as well: "I am more than how he treated me. I am not letting him take any more time away from me. No more time at appointments. No more time being afraid, and no more time being manipulated." For the full twenty minutes that Emma Ann spoke, her mother kept her eyes locked on Larry in a scalding gaze.

Afterward, Judge Aquilina heaped on the praise. "Your words are as strong as any gun, taser, or billy club. You need to keep on talking. You're very special. You are. Your sister survivor warriors stand with you," she told Emma Ann. "Your words, your advice, are as wise as any detective, lawyer, or prosecutor. Maybe one day I'll see you practice law in front of me. I don't know what your plans are, but you are going places."

She closed with these superb words, "Leave your pain here, and go out and do those magnificent things I know you were born to do."

Chapter Twenty-Two

The Courtroom

Larry Nassar never saw it coming. Sure, he agreed in his plea deal to let all the women who had reported his abuse speak in court. But he did not expect the colossal showdown that followed. In early 2018, over the course of nine days in two Michigan counties, more than two hundred women stood up and took back the power. They confronted him, exposed him, and emboldened each other—as well as countless others around the world—to speak out.

"It is a public courtroom," Judge Rosemarie Aquilina tells me. "I borrow the courtroom from the people. They have a right to speak in their courtroom to their elected judge and to the person who affected their life."

Her own personal journey to the Nassar case is a story of America.

The freethinking judge, known for wearing cowboy boots and red streaks in her black hair, is the daughter of a German mother and a Maltese father. She came to America from Germany as a baby with her mother, back in 1959. They lived with her paternal grandparents in Detroit, while her father finished medical school in Germany. "My grandfather was a tailor who worked for Henry Ford," she says. "My mother worked in a bank in downtown Detroit." As she entered kindergarten, her father came to the States, and the family moved around while he completed his medical internship and residency, eventually settling in Saginaw, Michigan, when she started the seventh grade. She was "very proud," she says, to become a naturalized citizen in 1968. "We were taught that we lived in the best place in the world."

At the same time, growing up in a European family in America, "I always felt different from others," she says. "I was not often listened to and was discounted, so I tended as I became an adult to listen more to others." In those early childhood years while the family moved around, "I rarely had friends and I never fit in," she says. "My siblings and books were my friends. I felt out of place because we had European values, traditions, accents, food, and had different sayings. I never felt accepted until high school. But I learned to adapt, and that served me well throughout my life."

She moved to East Lansing to attend Michigan State, where she majored in English and minored in journalism; then she went to law school at Western Michigan University. "I always wanted to be an author," she says, explaining the English major. "My father was concerned about me supporting myself. As a physician, he wanted me to also attend medical school, which I had no interest in." She went to law school instead, defying her strong-willed father, as she had done throughout her childhood. "I became a lawyer because of my constantly having to use my voice with my father and find my own path, which law allowed me to do, in addition to pursuing writing." She went on to write crime novels and serve for twenty years in the Army National Guard, becoming the first female judge advocate general, or JAG, in the state of Michigan. She has been serving as a circuit court judge since 2008 and was a district court judge for four years before that.

Her unique path to the bench, she tells me, has given her a broad perspective in her work.

At the Nassar sentencing hearing where the women gave their statements, she spoke personally and passionately to every single one of them. "I always speak to victims. I want them to know they have been heard and believed," she says. "I need them to feel and understand that they matter. The robe is powerful. They may not believe others who tell them they matter, but the power of the robe helps them to feel they are believed."

Larry Nassar's lawyers later accused her of bias because of her strong words for him in court, to which she says, "I was fair to both sides throughout the process, and at various times upset each side. That is a sign of a fair process." She points out that before the doctor pleaded guilty, when she was preparing the case for trial, she had upset the victims by putting a gag order on them, in an effort to be fair to the defendant.

Ultimately, after the doctor pleaded guilty, the women had the opposite of a gag order. "I allowed every victim to speak," Judge Aquilina says. She also let them speak for as long as they needed, with some speaking for thirty or forty minutes, facing down the predator who had upended their lives.

Emotions ran high in Judge Aquilina's Ingham County courtroom—for everyone involved, on all sides. During the sentencing hearing, distraught parents had to sit in the same room as the man who had abused their children. Women had to delve into their dark past as they confronted their betrayer. On the defense side, Shannon Smith, the Nassar attorney hired in the early days of the case, says she came under fire for representing him. "People were critical of me for being a woman and a mother and representing him," she says. "We were getting death threats. We put cameras at my office and around my home." She says that behind the scenes, she had advocated for a plea deal that would give the women a chance to speak in court. Later, at a second sentencing hearing in Eaton County, a devastated father lunged at Larry Nassar, after asking Judge Janice K. Cunningham for "five minutes in a locked room" with him. In the end, the survivors ruled the day, drawing attention from across the world. "The power of the victims was shared by each of them but extended to all those watching—especially victims who did not have a safe place to speak," Judge Aquilina tells me. "The fear of blame and shame dissipated as they saw others release their pain in my courtroom."

As the women kept standing up, one by one, others gained the strength to do so too.

That's what happened with Marion Siebert. A dancer who had grown up seeing Larry at the Michigan State clinic, she had written a statement and planned to have a victim advocate read it. Then she went to court and saw the very first survivor to speak, Kyle Stephens, the young woman who had grown up next door to Larry, suffering his abuse starting at age six when he exposed himself to her in the boiler room of his basement. "She just blew me away," Marion says, and she felt emboldened to stand up too. She happened to glance at her phone and saw that Kyle was already on the CNN homepage—before she even finished her statement. The world was watching. Soon after, Marion found herself walking up to the stand.

Her path to the podium is fascinating. For months, she tells me, she had tried to reconcile the pale, drawn sex offender in the news with the doctor she had known as a child, a man she had believed to be a caring person. "It was very disorienting," she says. She had remembered him as warm and funny, "good at making you like him, but not in the traditional charismatic way." She grappled with who he really was and what he had done. "One of the things I was struggling with for a long time was, Who is this person? Who is this human being that I know, this person from my past? I *knew* him. There's this whole cognitive dissonance thing." To help make it more real, she went to one of his child pornography court hearings, to see him in the flesh. "It was the first time I'd seen him in a long time," she says. "To see him was really conflicting, to see someone you know in pain, even if they deserve it. It's hard to see the truth and not be able to reconcile that. I started crying in the middle of all these people. But it became tangible to me."

Marion, who is now in her thirties, points out that it's not easy to go public as a survivor. She noted this in her statement, discussing the sacrifices the women have made in telling their stories. "They've had to publicly attach you—and what you did to them—to their names," she told Larry in court. "Every time someone googles them, possibly for the rest of our lives, they will see the sickening things we're talking about here today. When they apply for a job, when they go on a first date. They won't be able to be the ones to fully make the choice on when to talk to their kids about what happened to them."

Indeed, her point about parents resonated with the survivors who have children. When and how to tell the kids—before they see the stories about Mom online—are challenges for all the parents in this case. There are videos across the internet of the women in court, describing the abuse of their childhood. Those videos will be online forever.

Judge Aquilina, a mother of five, had some personal wisdom for the parents in her court.

Among them, Nicole Walker. Now in her thirties, she grew up in gymnastics, first meeting Larry when she was four years old at Great Lakes Gymnastics in the late eighties. When I sit down with her in Lansing, I can see the torment in her eyes. She has had a rough year, feeling isolated from friends who don't understand her trauma, and wondering how to tell her young son about the abuse of her past. "He's such a friendly kid," she says. "As a parent, what do you say?" She addressed that issue in her victim impact statement, persevering through the wave of disgust she felt at making eye contact with Larry, she tells me. She told the court about her parenting challenges, including the stress of taking her son to the doctor. She had grown up learning to trust doctors, but now, how could she tell her child to do the same?

"He had his first real exam a few months ago and was hesitant about letting the doctor pull his pants down to check for a hernia," she said in court, fighting back tears. "As I looked at his face, I could see that he was scared, and I couldn't help myself from crying, so I had to turn away. The doctor reassured him that he had nothing to worry about and that only a doctor should do this exam. Those words reassured him—as they should—but on the other hand, I felt extreme anxiety rush over my body. How do I ever explain this to my son? I should be able to tell him that it's OK, and he should be able to trust the doctors. But I don't trust anymore."

Judge Aquilina offered this heartfelt advice: "Here's something for you, mom to mom. He's robbed you of so much already. Don't let him rob you of enjoying your son, your family, your husband, your boyfriend, whoever is in your life. You were violated. Don't carry that violation into the next generation. Take your power back. Live happily with your child and your family, ma'am. I know you can do that. I've seen the spark in you. I think you're going to feel it again. Can you do that for me?"

Nicole replied, "I'm going to try my best."

Nicole met with me several months after her statement in court, and she was still trying.

It's a long road to recovery.

Megan Farnsworth faces the same challenge with her two kids. Her eyes well up as she tells me about it in Lansing, talking about her experience in depth for the first time outside her family. Megan, now in her thirties, was a gymnast on the team at Holt High School when Larry began abusing her. As an adult, she had been living a happy life with her family when the realization that she had been abused as a child came smashing into her world, causing her to descend into nightmares and flashbacks. She remembered how Larry had pulled out a medical book and told her how his "treatment" would help. She recalled a look on his face once when he treated her—a look of excitement. As a child, she had pushed it out of her mind. She also remembered talking to her sister and parents about his procedure. They advised her to tell him she was uncomfortable with it. She didn't feel she could say that to the Olympic doctor; she was just a kid. The memories stalked her. She questioned her younger self, her family. She wondered why she had placed her trust in the doctor. She questioned her parents and their advice at the time. Her mind spun.

Now, she says, "I have a seven-year-old and a three-year-old. When do I tell them? When is it appropriate? When do I tell my daughter? She needs to know." She tackled the issue in her victim impact statement, saying, "I will never be completely whole again. I have a daughter of my own that I will now worry too much over, and it is because of him." However, she added, Larry will not prevail. "He has to live with what he has done. He has to live with this forever, and even though there are parts of me that will always be affected by his actions, I get to walk away and know that I will be a better person because of it. I will be a better parent because of it. I can walk through life taking this with me and finding a way to grow from it."

As a private person and a parent, going public with her name in court was a big decision, but she's glad she did it, she says, noting that she is fortunate to have a supportive husband. Writing her statement, she could feel herself growing stronger, even though she was still reeling emotionally, tortured by the memories and questions. "I felt like this won't control me," she says. She tells me she did have one regret, though: she wished she had used her maiden name in her statement—Brooks—so Larry would remember her, since a victim advocate had read her statement in court. Megan says she had once considered Larry to be such a good friend, she had invited him to her high school graduation party. She wanted him to remember how he had deceived her. She wanted him to know she was stripping him of his power.

She was heartened to hear the words of encouragement from Judge Aquilina, who zoomed in on her feelings of never being whole again, saying, "Only a whole person could have written such a strong and wonderful statement."

Trinea Gonczar, the gymnast who got manipulated into taking ice baths at Larry's apartment as a child, was pregnant with a son when she made her way to the stand. She had vigorously defended Larry when the allegations emerged, believing his treatment to be legitimate, until the child pornography arrest helped her see the truth. At that point, he invaded her dreams, appearing in a recurring nightmare as a wolf devouring a girl in a warehouse, then turning his ravenous eyes on her. As she waited her turn in court, she tells me, Larry looked over and mouthed the words, "I'm so sorry. I'm so sorry." She thinks perhaps he was sorry that she had to see him in court, not sorry for anything he had done. The two had been lifelong friends. Trinea glared back, then stood and knocked him out with her words.

"What have you done? My words are to you, Larry. We both know I have known you basically all of my life. In fact, I've known you thirty-one of thirty-seven years, and this last year has traumatized me in ways you cannot even begin to imagine, as I have had to realize I was abused for many years of my life. And this, my old friend, is because of you." Then she shared her spine-chilling memories of moments they had shared. "I remember your wedding. I remember the laughs we would have in the back room at Great Lakes. I remember you taping my shins and my heels with such care and perfection." Her soulful parting words: "This is goodbye to you, Larry, and this time, it's time for me to close the door. It's time for me to stand up for these little girls and not stand behind you anymore, Larry. Goodbye, Larry. May God bless your dark, broken soul."

Judge Aquilina declared, "You're going to be an amazing mother, an amazing spokesperson. You turned this—I hate to call it friendship because it was only one-sided—but you've turned it into something good for others. And shutting the door on him is a prison door."

Boom.

When Trinea left the stand, Larry Nassar was openly sobbing—a rare display of emotion.

Chapter Twenty-Three

The Army of Survivors

On a June afternoon in Lansing, a small but powerful party assembles in a building across from the cast-iron dome of the state capitol. Judge Aquilina is here, looking sleek in black. A dozen survivors are here as well, including three who sounded the alarm on Larry over the years: Larissa Boyce, Amanda Thomashow, and Rachael Denhollander. All have become fierce advocates for women and girls. They have gathered for the signing of the legislation to give childhood sexual abuse victims more time to take legal action.

A handful of state lawmakers and lawyers mingle with politicos at the private event, sipping wine and hard apple cider. Judge Aquilina hangs out by an amazing array of cookies, cakes, and brownies. She recommends the mini glasses of mousse.

Attorney Jamie White, who wrote the legislation with state lawmakers, is here, as is Senator Margaret O'Brien, a lead sponsor. It was a challenge to get the law passed, amid pushback from the Catholic Church and other institutions that feared an expanded flow of lawsuits. Ultimately, the law didn't go as far as the survivors wanted, but it is a step, Senator O'Brien says. "I knew it wouldn't be an easy lift," she tells me. "You accomplish victories in steps, not leaps."

The new law is personal to everyone in the room. Larry Nassar put the Lansing community through hell. But a group of indomitable women brought him down. "He has emboldened the most powerful, determined, focused group of women you're ever going to meet," says attorney Jamie White. As for the community, it has been a jarring ordeal, he says, as the initial shock and disbelief turned to horror and a resounding call for accountability at Michigan State. "I hope the university ends up stronger," he says. "I think it will. A lot of mistakes were made. I think other universities will learn from watching this. And I still love this university." After all, it's his alma mater. He is now endowing a scholarship for a female athlete at the school.

As for Larry Nassar, he will spend the rest of his life behind bars, serving out his sentences for the child pornography as well as the criminal sexual conduct, which will keep him behind bars for at least one hundred years.

And the sister survivors will grow ever stronger.

They are watchdogs now. They keep an eye on Michigan State, USA Gymnastics, the US Olympic Committee, and many others. They're fighting for accountability and change—speaking out in the media, at Michigan State board meetings, at congressional hearings in Washington. And they're blasting officials when they blunder, which they often do.

Sarah Klein and Trinea Gonczar, the gymnasts who got manipulated into taking baths at Larry's apartment as children, are devoting themselves to helping people who have survived sexual assault: Sarah now serves as an attorney for survivors, while Trinea works for a nonprofit that provides resources and care.

Amanda Thomashow, the whistleblower who reported Larry to Michigan State and the police in 2014, to no avail, is now a campus sexual assault coordinator for a division of the Michigan Department of Health. When Larry finally got busted in 2016, she says, she felt vindicated but incredibly frustrated too; he could have been stopped two years earlier if she hadn't been gaslighted when she reported him. Now she is an outspoken activist, coining the phrase "army of survivors" when she confronted Larry in court: "The thing you didn't realize while you were sexually assaulting me and all of these young girls and breaking our lives is that you were also building an army of survivors who would ultimately expose you for what you truly are: a sexual predator. You might have broken us, but from this rubble we will rise as an army of female warriors."

Indeed. Jessica Howard, the three-time national champion rhythmic gymnast, is now an advocate for children's safety in sports, testifying before Congress, speaking on *60 Minutes*, penning an op-ed for the *New York Times*, and working with groups including Equality League, which trains athletes as advocates for the rights of women and girls in sports. The group's founder, Mara Gubuan, an advocate for women fighting against discrimination and sexual violence around the world, launched the group after seeing the Nassar survivors stand up in court. Jessica is a tremendous asset, Mara tells me, noting that when Jessica speaks at events, "she is both strong and vulnerable, leaving audiences shaken and inspired."

Jessica's new life as an activist has helped give her a purpose. "It is exactly what I wanted to do next. It gives me solace and peace," she says, noting that she draws inspiration from her fellow activists, including Equality League board members Minky Worden of Human Rights Watch and Nancy Hogshead-Makar, a three-time Olympic gold medalist swimmer, civil rights attorney, and founder of the advocacy group Champion Women. Nancy, who survived a campus rape in college, says she understands how crucial it is for survivors like Jessica to give themselves "permission to be vulnerable and heal." She learned that the hard way. After her own assault, she suffered from posttraumatic stress disorder but tried to push it away. "I made the mistake of telling myself, There's nothing to worry about here, you're fine," she tells me. "You need to follow your emotion. You need to let yourself feel it. Allow yourself to go down, and have faith that you will bounce back." That can be especially challenging for gymnasts who are taught to be tough, she notes, adding, "We expect our young athletes to be soldiers."

To be sure, the militant coaching in gymnastics needs a major overhaul—an issue the activists are tackling. Valorie Kondos Field, the former coach of the UCLA women's gymnastics team, notes that the change can start at home. "Instead of asking your kids, 'Did you win today?' You can ask, 'Did you learn anything today? What are your goals? How are you feeling?'" In other words, put the focus on the person, not the win. The same goes for coaches, she tells me. "It's so easy to play god to these kids. They'll do anything for you. Be a motivator, not a dictatorial ass."

Kayla Spicher is the coach of the future. At the Michigan gym where she coaches, Splitz Gymnastics, she took the time to sit down with her young athletes to explain the Nassar scandal swirling in the news. She encouraged them to speak up if something seems wrong—or even if nothing seems wrong and they just want to vent. Sitting with me in Lansing, the sparky twenty-three-year-old describes how she tailored her talks with the girls depending on their age, given the sensitive topic, but the upshot for everyone was: you have a voice.

She laughs when she recalls an eight-year-old saying, "I saw you on TV!" Indeed, Kayla had appeared on television, giving her victim impact statement in court. Her mother, also a gymnastics coach, stood tall beside her as Kayla spoke to Larry, a man she had known ever since she was a toddler. He broke down and cried as Kayla addressed him—one of his rare displays of emotion in court. Kayla notes that he often remained expressionless or shook his head as the women spoke, insinuating that he didn't know them or that they weren't telling the truth, which Kayla found tremendously disrespectful.

"Choosing to come out publicly was one of the hardest decisions I've ever faced," she told him. "I didn't want people to see me as broken. But I am not broken. I am strong—stronger than I've ever been. I chose to do this because no one should ever feel ashamed to come forward for help, advice, or just to have their voice heard."

At the reception for the bill signing, I meet another young leader of the movement, Grace French. A classically trained ballerina who is now a college student at the University of Michigan, she and her mother launched a project to tie shimmery teal bows around more than two hundred trees across the Michigan State campus, each with the name of a survivor. The bows, in the color of sexual assault awareness, became a powerful tribute around the leafy school grounds. Now the bows are in the Michigan State Museum, with curators working to preserve them for the permanent collection.

Grace has also founded an advocacy group, enlisting the help of fellow survivors, including Sara Teristi, the gymnast who may have been the very first victim of Larry Nassar, and Dr. Danielle Moore, the doctor of clinical and forensic psychology who once treated sex offenders before realizing she had been the target of a sex offender herself. The women came together from across the decades—from the very beginning of the Nassar saga to the very end—to launch the group, the Army of Survivors, which advocates for nationwide laws to shield athletes and others from sexual violence.

At the bill signing, Grace greets me with warmth and elegance; she is a dancer, with the posture of a heroine from a Jane Austen movie. Later she tells me a phenomenal story about her path to activism. She grew up loving the beauty and poetry of dance. She had begun taking ballet classes as a four-year-old, picturing herself becoming a professional dancer one day. At age twelve, when a schoolyard wrist injury landed her in Larry's office, she was impressed by the photos of the Olympians on the wall. "My goal was to be on his wall," she says. She saw him for dance-related injuries after that, and he began abusing her at the Michigan State clinic, as well as in the basement of the venue where her dance company performed, doing so behind closed curtains before she went onstage to perform. The "treatments" made her deeply uncomfortable. But Larry was the Olympic doctor. She trusted him, she tells me. She trusted that he was doing a medical procedure that would help her keep dancing.

When the Nassar scandal erupted, the news of the abuse sent her into a "disoriented" state of denial, she says. For months, she tried to ignore the news and go on with her life. Despite her discomfort, despite her experience, she couldn't yet accept that she herself had been abused. But when the survivors stood up in court to give their statements, she felt compelled to watch. Seeing the women take the stand, one after another, telling stories that mirrored her own, helped her understand the truth.

Acceptance, however, was only the beginning of a new phase of her life. Her embrace of the truth led to a dark spiral of flashbacks, nightmares, and panic attacks. Larry began raiding her sleep in a recurring nightmare, emerging from the darkness, pale and ghoulish, with sunken eyes—or no eyes at all. "In the dream, I'm in a dark room, and he appears and says, 'I need to treat you . . . I need to feel you,'" she tells me. The dream slammed her awake in a panic every time. "I would wake up and feel like he was coming out of the shadows in the room. It was like a blurring of reality."

The nightmares started coming so often, she could no longer sleep, knowing that sleep would only bring the nightmare again. With no rest at night, she struggled to stay awake in class during the day.

How does someone break such a spiral?

Grace made a simple yet profound change. And like so many of her fellow survivors, she carved her own path.

Grace found solace in a universal experience—something that people have taken comfort in through the ages. She got herself a dog, Bentley, and that has made the difference.

She trained Bentley to help her out at night, in the darkest of hours, in the most remarkable of ways. Now, when the nightmares begin, Bentley senses it and gently wakes her up. Then he sweeps the room, doing a safety patrol. She is teaching him how to turn on the lights now as well. He gives her a sense of security. He reduces her stress. He allows her to get much-needed sleep so she can live her life.

I find Grace's story particularly moving precisely because it is so universal. Over the past year, as I spoke with the twenty-five survivors who shared their stories in the pages of this book, many of whom, like Grace, had a difficult time accepting the truth of the abuse, it was fascinating to see the power of the mind—how it can go into self-protection mode and bury the pain but eventually find a way to come to terms with it. Grace's story speaks to that human ability to survive, adapt, and move forward.

For me, watching these women navigate a reality that nobody would have chosen has been truly inspiring. They are the embodiment of power.

Their story is the triumph of the human spirit.

While I was wrapping up the book on a recent evening, thinking about the extraordinary people I had met during this project, Grace French emailed me a picture of herself with Bentley, hanging out together on the south shore of Lake Superior on an autumn day in Michigan. In the photo, she and her boyfriend have hoisted an oversized Bentley—he's a springer spaniel and poodle mix, with the face of a puppy who looks like he doesn't quite realize he's a giant dog—up in their arms for a snapshot. It takes both of them to lift him. Grace is smiling. And so is Bentley.

Like so many of the women I've met, they have found their path forward, together.

Acknowledgments

Thank you to the survivors and their families for trusting me with their stories.

Thank you to Joel Oestreich for his unwavering love and support throughout this project.

A special thanks to my creative and ever-supportive family: John Pesta, an author and former newspaper publisher who taught me the art of storytelling—and encouraged me to do my own thing; Maureen O'Hara Pesta, an artist who finds timeless beauty in quiet moments and memories and always brings me calm; and Jesse Pesta, a globetrotting writer, photographer, and an editor at the *New York Times* whose advice on this book and on so many things is immeasurable.

Many thanks to my agent, Lynn Johnston, for seeing the power in this story, and to my editor at Seal Press, Stephanie Knapp, and publisher Lara Heimert for giving the women in these pages a powerful platform. And thanks to the entire team that worked with me on the book, including Laura Mazer, Sharon Kunz, Liz Wetzel, Nancy Sheppard, Allison Finkel, Megan Schindele, Elisa Rivlin, and many others.

Cheers to Jamie White, Judge Rosemarie Aquilina, Michelle Tuegel, Mara Gubuan, Minky Worden, Nancy Hogshead-Makar,

Senator Margaret O'Brien, Andrew Abood, Jim Graves, Mick Grewal, and Valorie Kondos Field for sharing their insights for this book.

A big thanks to Sheila Weller, Laurie Sandell, Michael Wright, Michele Shapiro, Samantha Marshall, Bill Holstein, and Allan Dodds Frank for their stellar advice on all things publishing.

Thank you to Joanna Coles, an inspiration to journalists who aspire to think outside the box, and to Tina Brown and her team at Women in the World for putting women center stage—and for introducing me to the wonderful Sandra Uwiringiyimana, my coauthor on the book *How Dare the Sun Rise*. Thank you to Paul Steiger for his encouragement and support, and to Cindi Leive for helping me carve out a beat I love. Many thanks to all the editors who have helped me tell powerful stories, including Kayla Adler, Miriam Arond, Sara Austin, Emma Barker, Lauren Smith Brody, Laura Brounstein, Alison Brower, Meredith Bryan, Joyce Chang, Marisa Cohen, Katie Connor, Riza Cruz, Pip Cummings, Kara Cutruzzula, Roe D'Angelo, Deidre Depke, Mike Elek, Rosemary Ellis, Edward Felsenthal, Lori Fradkin, Anne Fulenwider, Lea Goldman, Susan Goodall, Jill Herzig, Noelle Howey, Lauren Iannotti, Susy Jackson, Rich Jaroslovsky, Whitney Joiner, Ellen Kampinsky, Lucy Kaylin, Marina Khidekel, Ellen Levine, Dave Mann, Danielle McNally, Tracy Middleton, Marty Munson, Wendy Naugle, John Nagy, Ezra Palmer, Jessica Pels, Michele Promaulayko, Geraldine Sealey, Harry Siegel, Kurt Soller, Jane Spencer, Sade Strehlke, Tim Taliaferro, Andrew Tavani, Kerry Temple, Tunku Varadarajan, Tom Weber, Lauren Williams, and Leslie Yazel, among many others.

Notes

1. Mark Alesia, Tim Evans, and Marisa Kwiatkowski, "Larry Nassar's Downfall Started with an Email to IndyStar," *IndyStar*, December 7, 2017.

2. Rebecca Davis O'Brien, "U.S. Investigates FBI Response to Gymnasts' Sex-Abuse Claims," *Wall Street Journal*, September 4, 2018.

3. Mark Alesia, Marisa Kwiatkowski, and Tim Evans, "Timeline: Former USA Gymnastics Doctor Larry Nassar," *IndyStar*, September 20, 2016.

4. Mark Alesia, Marisa Kwiatkowski, and Tim Evans, "Timeline: Former USA Gymnastics Doctor Larry Nassar," *IndyStar*, September 20, 2016.

5. Mark Alesia, Marisa Kwiatkowski, and Tim Evans, "Timeline: Former USA Gymnastics Doctor Larry Nassar," *IndyStar*, September 20, 2016.

6. Eric Lacy and Christopher Haxel, "Accomplished, Controversial Coach," *Lansing State Journal*, February 9, 2018.

7. Coverage by the *Lansing State Journal* and *IndyStar* of the USAToday Network, "Who Is Larry Nassar?" (undated timeline of Nassar's career), https://www.usatoday.com/pages/interactives/larry-nassar-timeline/.

8. Charles E. Ramirez, "Psychologist in Nassar Case Surrenders License," *Detroit News*, September 28, 2018.

9. Eric Lacy and Christopher Haxel, "Accomplished, Controversial Coach," *Lansing State Journal*, February 9, 2018.

10. Sarah Fitzpatrick and Tracy Connor, "McKayla Maroney Says She Tried to Raise Sex Abuse Alarm in 2011," NBCNews.com, April 22, 2018, https://www.nbcnews.com/news/us-news/mckayla-maroney-says-she-tried-raise-sex-abuse-alarm-2011-n867911.

11. Eric Lacy and Christopher Haxel, "Accomplished, Controversial Coach," *Lansing State Journal*, February 9, 2018.

12. Matt Mencarini, "MSU Let Larry Nassar See Patients for 16 Months During Criminal Sexual Assault Investigation," *Lansing State Journal*, December 20, 2017.

13. Tracy Connor, Sarah Fitzpatrick, and Kenzi Abou-Sabe, "Silent No More," NBCNews.com, April 23, 2018, https://www.nbcnews.com /news/us-news/silent-no-more-inside-usa-gymnastics-sex-abuse -scandal-n868221.

14. Mark Alesia, Marisa Kwiatkowski, and Tim Evans, "Timeline: Former USA Gymnastics Doctor Larry Nassar," *IndyStar*, September 20, 2016.

15. Rebecca Davis O'Brien, "U.S. Investigates FBI Response to Gymnasts' Sex-Abuse Claims," *Wall Street Journal*, September 4, 2018.

Jesse Pesta

Abigail Pesta is an award-winning journalist and author who has lived and worked around the world, from London to Hong Kong. She is the coauthor of *How Dare the Sun Rise: Memoirs of a War Child*, which was named among the best books of 2017 by the New York Public Library, the Chicago Public Library, and many others; the *New York Times* calls it a "gut-wrenching, poetic memoir." Her investigative and feature reporting has appeared in major media outlets, including the *Wall Street Journal*, the *New York Times*, *New York Magazine*, *Cosmopolitan*, *The Atlantic*, *Marie Claire*, *Newsweek*, *Glamour*, and NBC News, among many others. She lives in Brooklyn, New York.